Essentials of Literary Criticism

Philip Hobsbaum

Essentials of
Literary Criticism

THAMES AND HUDSON

*For my dear step-daughters, Jane and Mary,
who stand for all the students I have taught
and from whom I have sought to learn*

© 1983 Thames and Hudson Ltd, London

First published in the United States of America in 1993 by
Thames and Hudson Inc., 500 Fifth Avenue,
New York, New York 10110

Library of Congress Catalog Card Number 93-60422

ISBN 0-500-27285-9

Printed and bound in Slovenia

Contents

Preface   7

  I The use of criticism   9 – 10

 II What to say about a poem   18

III Four modes of fiction   35 – 19

 IV English prose style   53

  V Writing notes   67 – 14

 VI Structuring an essay   80 –

VII Background and biography   98 – 15

VIII Comparison and analysis   111 – 20

 IX The model essay / Breaking the model   131 – 13

Bibliography   143

Index   147

'The critic's perceptions and judgments are his, or they are nothing; but, whether or not he has consciously addressed himself to co-operative labour, they are inevitably collaborative. Collaboration may take the form of disagreement, and one is grateful to the critic whom one has found worth disagreeing with'

F. R. Leavis, *The Common Pursuit*

'The Text requires an attempt to abolish (or at least to lessen) the distance between writing and reading, not by intensifying the reader's projection into the work, but by linking the two together in a single signifying process'

Roland Barthes, 'From Work to Text'

Preface

The purpose of this book is to provide a guide to the detailed discussion of literary texts. Primarily it is designed for the first-year university student, though it should also be found useful in the later stages of secondary or high school. It could also be used by school and university teachers with their classes.

The basic procedure is to examine specific passages in the first four chapters, arranged according to genre, and in chapters 5 – 8 to put them in a larger context, at the same time suggesting approaches that the student could take in writing about them. The last chapter consolidates previous remarks on the writing of the critical essay: the form in which, for better or worse, students of English Literature are required to express themselves. My reason for undertaking the book is that, as far as I am aware, it is the first to place as much emphasis on writing about literature as on reading it.

I wish to thank my wife for her inexhaustible patience during the writing of this book; my university, and especially its great library, for help without which nothing could have been done; my teachers and students, for all I have learned from them; and my departmental secretary, Mrs Valerie Eden, whose skill in her craft helped to consolidate my work.

I The use of criticism

One's first reaction to a work of literature is instinctive and emotional. Yet this reaction implies within it the judgement that would be evident in any reasoned account we should later give of the text. Strictly speaking, what we do in giving such an account is not so much analyse the text as our reaction to it. This is a useful thing to do because, unless we rationalize our feelings, we cannot be certain whether our reaction is a just one or not. Further, it gives us a chance to check our judgement against that of colleagues or other critics. Such a check may act as a safeguard against misreading or prejudice. Ultimately the reasons given for holding an opinion are as important as the opinion itself.

Alone in the field of the arts it is possible to speak of literary criticism in terms of progress. Roughly speaking, criticism has been tied up with the development of science and of analytical philosophy. It had its first flowering in Ancient Greece when Aristotle described the key dramas of his time, and it suffered grave setbacks in the Dark Ages of the medieval period.

This does not mean that criticism is a branch of science. It does not present factual proof so much as demonstrate a point of view. But the language in which it couches that demonstration resembles that of the more analytical forms of philosophy. Therefore criticism in English has been dependent upon the development of scientific prose. Thus the critical views of Sir Philip Sidney are obscured by the rhetoric in the only form of prose open to him in the sixteenth century. John Dryden, however, wrote concurrently with the foundation of the Royal Society. His prose bears traces of the conceptual logic necessary for the description of scientific experiment and is, accordingly, all the more lucid a medium for critical discussion.

Nevertheless, like most critics, Dryden was essentially a debater. Criticism seems always most to have flourished when an old order was to be defended or a new one evinced. At its best it always has the smack of urgency. We find in the eighteenth century Dr Johnson gravely reproving Romantic incursions upon the neo-classical decorum of his time. Half a century later, Wordsworth and Coleridge produced the manifesto for what their contemporaries felt was a poetic revolution. More than sixty years after, Matthew Arnold combined the high-minded academicism of Johnson with the distrust of convention shown by Wordsworth and Coleridge. His concern for the education of personal sensibility set the central line of criticism in the twentieth century. The highly analytical prose of I.A. Richards and T.S. Eliot was developed out of Coleridge and Arnold to defend the modern poetry which was, in the 1920s, heavily under fire. F.R. Leavis and William Empson showed how the approach could work retrospectively, adapting itself to the discussion of works of the past. Their mode of criticism is itself part of a new development in the twentieth century, the academic teaching of English literature. This in its turn produced a cautious attempt at consolidation, if not retrenchment, in the 1950s and 1960s. A primary form was Historical Intentionalism, whereby the critic attempted to reconstruct the work of literature to give some idea of how its readers saw it at the time of publication. This diminished the need for personal judgement. But such caution was no doubt a result of the way in which the practice of criticism had outrun in the present century any possible theory upon which it could be based. An overhaul of literary theory, initiated mostly from France, occurred in the 1970s. As a result of this, criticism took another step forward and now emerged as a key area of thought. The new movement was called Structuralism and derives from the practice of such figures as the anthropologist, Claude Lévi-Strauss, and the historian, Michel Foucault. These writers laid great emphasis on cultural patterns as a determinant of human behaviour. In terms of criticism, this means that we should take into account our own historical standpoint at the time of reading a work of literature, as well as the historical character of the period when it was first produced.

With all this development there is no excuse for failing to write a lucid and persuasive prose. Earlier critics had the disadvantage of coping with concepts that were still nascent, and the prose of Leavis or Blackmur, for instance, sometimes bears signs of that struggle. The best models are often found not in criticism but in the less exacting field of moral and analytical philosophy. Russell, and his disciples Ryle and Ayer, are good examples of how an argument can be set out plainly. All three, for instance, characteristically allow only one idea per sentence: a rule that makes for brevity and precision.

Related to this is the nature of critical argument itself. Of necessity it must be a selection from the manifold points of view open to the educated sensibility. The critic should select the line of argument that seems to him most germane to his reaction to the text, and he should follow it through rigorously without being diverted into parenthetic by-ways, no matter how beguiling they may seem. Diversions and parentheses obscure argument. It is much better to get one idea across than to hint at and fail to grasp a dozen others.

Every statement should be backed up by an example and every example should be further defined by a relevant comment. Otherwise the reader has no way of accurately gauging the critic's point of view.

Each point should arise logically out of the point made before it. This can be most easily checked by classifying individual points under various heads; alphabetical letters would do. If all the A's and B's aggregate together and are followed by C's and D's, well and good. The system may seem absurdly simple, but few critical essays would stand up against an analysis couched on these lines.

The object of criticism is to describe the work and to persuade the reader that the description is valid. Therefore precision of fact, vocabulary and argument is of the very essence. You cannot have any sort of a discussion if your adversary is not fully conversant with his opponent's point of view.

The most common mistake I find among my students is their frequent belief that a work of literature cannot be discussed. There is a built-in paradox here. Even when they claim a work is not discussible they are, in a sense, discussing it. But to claim the standpoint of total subjectivity is to discount all possibility of criticism, of teaching, of education altogether.

Some students indeed even claim that a work *ought* not to be discussed. But surely it is clear that discussion and analysis are likely to give rise to a deeper appreciation of its quality. Only a bad work is likely to suffer from close attention.

Another aberration I have had occasion to correct is a too literal rendering of the work. This usually takes the form of plot-summary. Retailing the events of a play or novel is not enough: one requires some act of interpretation, of appreciation. Otherwise criticism becomes indistinguishable from mechanical exercise such as précis.

At the other extreme is the error of the wandering argument. It is surprising how few students sketch out their line of argument beforehand. First-year students, in particular, tend to work by an associative method whereby one idea gives rise to another and the essay meanders further and further away from its original point.

Allied to this is the tendency to respond to a specific question with an answer that was not called for; to give answers, in fact, that are irrelevant. Even in a general essay one should take up a definite stand to which all points made in the essay should relate.

These are only a few of the errors that abound, but they all have a family resemblance. Subjectivism, incoherence, irrelevance and inconclusiveness are still the chief weaknesses of modern critical writing.

In spite of this, it is in the area of terminology that criticism may be seen most clearly to have advanced in the twentieth century. Nobody would wish a critical essay to be heavily technical in the way a scientific paper must necessarily be; at the same time it is obvious that any extension of our critical vocabulary gives us access to a greater delicacy of description than would otherwise be the case.

Characteristically terminology is extended by the activities of a major critic or theorist. Thus to Richards we owe the terms, in their current usage, 'tone', 'intention', 'effect', 'sense', 'feeling'. To Eliot we owe 'dissociation of sensibility', 'objective correlative'; to Leavis 'concreteness', 'realization', 'enactment'; to Empson 'ambiguity', 'double plot'; to Winters 'qualitative progression', 'imitative form'; to Lévi-Strauss 'bricolage'; to Foucault 'episteme'; to Shklovsky 'defamiliarization' or *ostranenie;* to Mukařovský 'foregrounding'.

Many of these were terms current in one form or another before they were taken up by the critics with whom they are now associated. But it was these critics who gave them their present application. Clearly it would be foolish to stuff an essay full of such terms, whether to show modernity or knowledge: critical terms should be the instruments of a critic's individual sensibility. But equally clearly it would be the height of ignorance to write as though the great critics had never improved on existing terminology. Criticism is a progressive form of description: it has deepened and broadened considerably in the twentieth century. No other form of enquiry would expect its new entrants to jettison all that had been with great pains studied out by their predecessors.

Literature is basically not feeling, thought or judgement; literature is words. At least the words are what, initially, we must point to. We certainly recognize that the discussion of a book on a purely verbal level will not take us very far; at the same time we must concede that any larger account of a given text represents something of an extrapolation.

I am far from saying that all literature must be discussed solely in terms of the language it uses. But some such analysis must take place, on or off the critic's printed page, if he is to proceed to larger terms. Otherwise those terms need not be valid: if the language is not effective, and seen to be so, there is no safeguard against reading into a badly written text our own private fantasies.

The process of analysis is necessarily highly selective: otherwise we would be faced with a discussion of a text many times longer than the original text itself. But the points selected for discussion should be the salient ones necessary for sustaining a critical argument, and behind each one should be the pressure of implication that indicates each example to be not only particular but representative.

At its best, as in the work of Empson, Leavis, James Smith and Douglas Brown, analysis can take us further into the work than could have been predicated of the act itself.

More than verbal analysis, the survey of form and structure is still in process of development. This is because the discussion of literature has so far dealt mainly with poetry and this lends itself readily to the analysis of language. Larger forms such as tragedy and the novel respond at least equally well to the description of structure. For example, Wilson Knight has shown how given images or themes hunt each other through the plays of Shakespeare. It could also be demonstrated that Jane Austen grounds her novels very much on patterns of human behaviour: children picking up bad habits from their parents, or siblings reacting against each other.

The survey of even larger issues is possible: Joseph Conrad's use of pause and parenthesis in plot, for example, or Henry James's technique of the withheld piece of information. It seems to me that this is the area in practical criticism that most is in process of amplification.

The great critics – Wilson Knight and Winters among them – have shown that it is possible to assess a story in such a way as to imply a very definite judgement upon it. This is what I should call interpretation, as distinct from plot-summary. It has a tripartite faculty: it conveys necessary information regarding the subject of a book, it indicates what the pattern of events actually signifies, and it conveys the feel and atmosphere of the text under survey. This last is especially important if one is to persuade an unconversant reader that one's chosen author is worthy of attention. Roughly it may be said that the better a work is, the more we are impelled from analysis into interpretation.

There is no way of writing criticism without in some manner implying judgement of value. Therefore it is best to be sure what one's judgement is and to make it as clear to the reader as possible. This will not seem arrogant on the part of a young critic if we remember that what he probes is his personal experience of the work in question. It is true that he is unlikely to write so well as Shakespeare or Pope, but this need not inhibit him from having a reaction to their work.

A word of warning is due here. Since we are all biologically similar, it may seem that those of us brought up in Western society are likely to have a fairly similar reaction to work that is good. It is true that, by very definition, work that is bad fails to communicate. But failure in communication can also be the fault of an inattentive reader. Very often when we attack a given work we are simply describing that which we have failed to understand. In other words, it is very hard to have a critical discussion about a work which offers no purchase to the reader. A cautious analysis rather than wholesale denunciation should be the order of the day. But such analysis is worth attempting because it may expose valid aspects of the work that a first reading would hastily pass over, and it does help critics who may not agree with one's view to see exactly why it is that one holds it. The reasons for holding a judgement often act as a way of defining that judgement more closely.

It is worthwhile putting in order one's view of a work because nothing in the long run is so bad for critical judgement as wholesale acceptance of inferior work. Clumsily written or obscure literature requires the reader to do a great deal of reading-in or mental rewriting. This is all very well in dealing with inferior

literature but deflects one badly when approaching a masterpiece
which requires no such over-active reading. The critic's duty is
to see and to describe what he sees. Description of what he can
dredge up out of his sub-consciousness forms no part of his
duty. Judgement is formed by comparisons; and, once judgement is reasonably formed, the critic is able to indicate some
kind of a hierarchy of existing works of literature, from those
which are ever-present classics through those of a secondary or
conventional order down to those which are so badly written as
to be scarcely present to the consciousness at all.

The critic's duty is to keep communications open between
reader and writer, the present and the past, and also to indicate
what of that past needs most attention in our own time; to keep,
in fact, the classics before our eyes. A related duty is to discrimi-
nate among the masses of books being produced at this present
moment in order to ensure that the best work gets a fair hearing.
To do all this requires a highly developed sense of value.

It could be argued that all of the seminal minds were literary
critics. Obviously this is so of the great writers, otherwise they
could not have done their work, but it was equally true of Marx,
Freud, Weber, Frazer and Trotsky. In our own time, it is true of
Lévi-Strauss and Foucault. Sensitivity to literary texts is a prime
requirement for those who would be at the creative front of what
is still a highly verbal society.

The term literary texts in the present argument may be held to
include political propaganda, newspapers, advertisements,
films, conceptual prose of all kinds, as well as literature proper.
If we are to avoid undue indoctrination, it will be necessary for
us to instruct as many readers as possible in the art of reading;
to inculcate, in fact, the critical spirit. Otherwise a great deal of
evasive rhetoric, operating for reasons of self-interest on the part
of the 'writer', will be accepted as fact and reason – with potenti-
ally disastrous consequences.

Moreover, it is essential that we all know something of how
language is used. In the absence of a once highly literate élite,
the need to preserve and develop the best in linguistic tradition

to some extent devolves upon each one of us. But our capacity to recognize excellence will be considerably impaired if we yield uncritically to the blandishments of inferior 'literature' – oratory, propaganda, advertising and the like.

Thus the training of a critic is also the training of a citizen: to judge political propaganda and commercial rhetoric no less than to choose material for personal enlightenment and entertainment. The study of criticism is the study of language in action. In a verbal society, this entails the study of civilization itself.

II What to say about a poem

A person may like and understand a poem and yet still have little idea of what can be said about it. Nevertheless, he may find himself required to write a critical essay with some such title as 'Wyatt's work is essentially a poetry of anger' or 'Herbert is one of the truly devotional poets of English literature'. Such an essay, whatever its incidentals, must rest on a substratum of critical analysis.

One's reaction to a poem is necessarily personal, but it can to some extent be rationalized. This rationalization can be very useful in showing another person where you stand. Essentially, critical discussion demonstrates a point of view. Your reader may not, in the end, choose to agree with you, but at least he knows your position. It is possible for me to indicate something of what I see in the poem I am about to quote; and this is the process we call critical analysis or critical discussion.

> They flee from me, that sometime did me seek
>   With naked foot, stalking in my chamber.
> I have seen them gentle, tame, and meek,
>   That now are wild, and do not remember
>   That sometime they put themselves in danger
>   To take bread at my hand; and now they range
>   Busily seeking with a continual change.
>
> Thanked be fortune it hath been otherwise
>   Twenty times better; but once, in special,
> In thin array, after a pleasant guise,

When her loose gown from her shoulders did fall,
And she me caught in her arms long and small,
　Therewith all sweetly did me kiss
　And softly said, 'Dear heart how like you this?'

It was no dream; I lay broad waking:
　But all is turned, through my gentleness,
Into a strange fashion of forsaking;
　And I have leave to go of her goodness,
　And she also to use newfangleness.
　　But since that I so kindly am served,
　　I would fain know what she hath deserved.

SIR THOMAS WYATT

Analysis is a term we adopt in criticism, but it is an analogy rather than a description. What we do is to analyse not the poem itself but its effect upon us. Since this effect tends to be a fairly complex one, it can be broken down into various parts; hence the term analysis. But we must remember that the analogy does not go very far. The poem on the page can be appreciated only in so far as it reacts with our ideas and feelings, and affects them.

In 'They flee from me' by Wyatt I would ask you to look out for what may be called the centre of the poem. This need not be a matter of geography: the 'centre' is as likely to be near the beginning or at the end as half-way through. The 'centre' is that which essentially gives the poem its identity. In any work, some parts are more crucial than others, and there usually is a climactic point when one has to say 'If anywhere, it is on this that the poem depends'. In the Wyatt poem, such a point may be found in stanza 2.

...In thin array, after a pleasant guise,
　When her loose gown from her shoulders did fall,
　And she me caught in her arms long and small,
　　Therewith all sweetly did me kiss
　　And softly said, 'Dear heart how like you this?'

In contrast to the rest of the poem, this is sharply seen. There is a high degree of actuality in such phrases as 'thin array', 'loose gown', 'arms long and small'. Not any gown is in question; not any arms. The adjectives limit and so define the characteristics of this mysterious lady. This concreteness, as we may call it, serves as a guarantee that the event happened; it enables us to suspend our disbelief.

The poem goes on to assert 'It was no dream'. Yet in the context of the poem the vividness of this incident has a dreamlike quality. This is not because the event is illusory but because it stands out in marked contrast to the less focused poetry of the whole. After all, the poem does not begin with sharp actuality –

> They flee from me, that sometime did me seek.

Who are 'they'? The term is uncomfortably inclusive, and well it may be, for the word 'they' is qualified by a dependent clause, 'that sometime did me seek'. This suggests that all who once sought the speaker now flee from him. The details that flesh out this inclusive concept, 'they', suggest nothing central to the experience. Rather they have a tentative, hesitating quality, like movements seen out of the corner of one's eye. 'They' have naked feet; 'they' used to stalk in the speaker's chamber; 'they' were once gentle, tame and meek – these details hint at birds, pets, children, dependents, lovers even. But at no point do they commit the poem or the reader to an explicit statement of fact. This effect, frequent in English poetry, is called 'ambiguity'. In the words of Sir William Empson, 'The fundamental situation is that a word or a grammatical structure is effective in several ways at once'. It is the combination of different areas of meaning in such a way as to imply some part of each of them. In this case, the total effect is that of desertion and that, essentially, is what the poem is about. Everything that the speaker loved and trusted has gone away.

Now we can see the second stanza in perspective. The tense changes, from the uncertain present of the beginning to a narrative concerned with an historical past. The speaker recapitulates one event he is able to grasp, if only in recollection. It is an event whose vividness is a guarantee that it happened. Once, things were better; once he, the speaker, now deserted, was sought out, caught, held, caressed. This recollection gives him a kind of fortitude with which to contemplate a desolate present time. In the last stanza he is able to understand his position with more distinctness. From the dispersed anxieties of the first stanza, when all we have is a general sense of withdrawal and consequent desolation, we move to the concentrated anger of the third stanza, focused upon one particular betrayal. The speaker thus lays down a basis for self-justification. The poem does not conclude on a hopeful note, but at least it is able to come to some conclusion –

> But since that I so kindly am served,
> I would fain know what she hath deserved.

He has been treated in this kind; treated 'kindly' only in a blackly ironic sense. But if he has been served in this way, justice would demand that 'she' – this she who has deserted him – should be served badly as well. Such is (a further ambiguity here) her desert!

My discussion has not yet encompassed all that takes place in the poem: for example, I have not considered the allegorical possibility that the Lady is a representation of Fortune. But then, no single analysis can contain a poem, and it should not even make the attempt. You can raise in class discussion such other possibilities as occur to you. What I was concerned to do here was to show a way into the poem; an approach by way of locating the poem's centre.

This approach would do, too, for the next poem we are to discuss; but, in this case, we can add a further consideration to our analysis.

THE PULLEY

> When God at first made Man,
> Having a glass of blessings standing by –

> Let us (said He) pour on him all we can;
> Let the world's riches, which dispersed lie,
>   Contract into a span.
>
> So strength first made a way,
> Then beauty flow'd, then wisdom, honour, pleasure:
> When almost all was out, God made a stay,
> Perceiving that, alone of all His treasure,
>   Rest in the bottom lay.
>
> For if I should (said He)
> Bestow this jewel also on My creature
> He would adore My gifts instead of Me,
> And rest in Nature, not the God of Nature:
>   So both should losers be.
>
> Yet let him keep the rest.
> But keep them with repining restlessness;
> Let him be rich and weary, that at least,
> If goodness lead him not, yet weariness
>   May toss him to My breast.

GEORGE HERBERT

If we start off looking for the centre, I think we shall find it here –

> Perceiving that, alone of all His treasure,
>   Rest in the bottom lay.

Unlike Wyatt, Herbert's point of climax coincides with his highest degree of ambiguity. There is a real pun here: rest remains at the bottom of God's tumbler. This is appropriate: rest is inert, when one rests one lies reposefully, when one is resting one does not put out an appreciable degree of energy or movement. So the concept of rest is made actual by showing it as the last blessing to fall from the glass. But in this inheres the allegorical meaning of the poem. The last blessing to be conferred upon man will be not only the latest but the rarest.

The word 'rest' is not allowed to remain in that position, at the bottom of a tumbler. It plays what amounts to a dramatic role through the poem, showing this apparently inert concept in different guises.

> [man would] rest in Nature, not the God of Nature.

Further to the residual idea of rest as repose on earth, we have the additional identification of rest as trust in God. The two ideas, indeed, are contrasted. So the line can be glossed as follows: left to himself, man would take his ease in worldly repose rather than seeking beyond material objects to the peace that resides in God, and is alone to be trusted.

Or again –

> Yet let him keep the rest
> But keep them with repining restlessness...

The use of the word 'rest' here is ironic; a new dimension has been added; an extra range of ambiguity. If man keeps the rest of the blessings, he still will find himself without the rest – the only rest worth having, rest not measurable in terms of worldly blessings, that rest which is the peace of God. Moreover in so far as 'rest' occurs in the word 'restlessness', it makes the absence of rest an entity, turning a negative attribute into a very real sense of unease. This unease melts into that disease that assails the proprietors of worldly blessings – weariness. It is the same weariness that, God says,

> May toss him to My breast.

The word 'toss' suggests a metaphor drawn from shipwreck. Nevertheless, the poem ends on a qualified note of hope. The greatest misfortune – total shipwreck, even – may lead to the greatest fortune of all, a fortune not to be estimated in worldly terms; union with God.

Our consideration of the poem's centre has, in this way, led us into a discussion of language. As we have seen, the language of this poem is both appropriate to its subject-matter and vivid in itself. This can be located especially in the verbs. Rest, appropriately enough, lay in the bottom of the glass. With equal appropriateness –

strength first made a way...

The blessing first out is the strongest; being strong, strength is able to force a way through, to make a way.

Then beauty flowed...

'Flowed' is a word used to describe the movement of rivers, the glitter of robes, the line of an accomplished dancer. Appropriateness such as this runs through the stanza; indeed, throughout the entire poem.

The language needs to be appropriate because, if it were less effective, the poem would be little more than a sermon. As such, it would appeal probably only to those already converted; it would be about God, not man. 'The Pulley' is, after all, based on an abstract concept; the idea of man being gifted and also self-destructive. If one is to act this idea out, rather than to sermonize around it, some kind of narrative technique in language is necessary. The poem is couched in a form which has its basis in the Bible: the parable. Like the story of the Prodigal Son, and that of the Good Samaritan, 'The Pulley' is a short story that, in its acting out, conveys a moral lesson.

After the storms of the seventeenth century we have, in the eighteenth century, what has been called the Peace of the Augustans. This did not mean that emotions were wiped away. Rather it suggested restraint, poise, the sober arrangement of one's feelings. If you read this next poem carefully, you will see that it exhibits the sort of control that a man has to assert if he is very angry indeed.

ATTICUS

Were there One whose fires
True Genius kindles, and fair Fame inspires;
Blest with each talent and each art to please,
And born to write, converse, and live with ease:
Should such a man, too fond to rule alone,   5
Bear, like the Turk, no brother near the throne,
View him with scornful, yet with jealous eyes,

> And hate for arts that caus'd himself to rise;
> Damn with faint praise, assent with civil leer,
> And without sneering, teach the rest to sneer;   10
> Willing to wound, and yet afraid to strike,
> Just hint a fault, and hesitate dislike;
> Alike reserv'd to blame, or to commend,
> A tim'rous foe, and a suspicious friend;
> Dreading ev'n fools, by Flatterers besieged,   15
> And so obliging, that he ne'er oblig'd;
> Like Cato, give his little Senate laws,
> And sit attentive to his own applause;
> While Wits and Templars ev'ry sentence raise,
> And wonder with a foolish face of praise:-   20
> Who but must laugh, if such a man there be?
> Who would not weep, if ATTICUS were he?

ALEXANDER POPE

Strictly speaking, this is not a separate poem but an extract from a larger work. But it was originally written as an independent piece and was only later incorporated in 'The Epistle to Dr Arbuthnot'. Therefore we shall for the moment look at it as an entity on its own. We shall have a chance of putting it into a larger context later on, in Chapter 5.

The centre of Atticus occurs right at the end –

> Who but must laugh, if such a man there be?
> Who would not weep, if ATTICUS were he?

This raises the question of tone – that ideal speaking voice which we assume when we read the poem aloud or hear it in our heads, as we should, when reading it silently. The tone is that of conversation – formal and ordered, but still conversation. It is the voice of a cultivated man of the world. He tells us about an acquaintance of his – a former friend, it would seem – and his earliest words assure us that this personage is a man to be reckoned with. Here we must also consider the appropriateness of the language. In the earliest lines, as I indicated, we have a vocabulary of praise: the man has genius, he has talent, he has art, he was

born to live with ease. But even though this is praise, it is praise
in a descending scale of enthusiasm. We move from 'genius' to
'ease', in fact. This Atticus, it would seem, takes life too easily.
And, as the praise diminishes, the blame comes in (lines 5–8) in
words like 'scornful', 'jealous', 'hate'. Out of context, this might
suggest an access of rage on the part of the speaker. But in context control is never lost; the suave tone prevails; we are sure of
five stresses to a line and we always find a rhyme at the end of
the couplet. More important still, in the next section (9–16) a
third area of language asserts itself. This Atticus does not damn
outright; there would be boldness in that, and he is circumspect;
he damns 'with faint praise'. Atticus does not wound; that
would show antagonism of an open kind; the will is there, but
not the performance –

> Willing to wound, and yet afraid to strike,
> Just hint a fault, and hesitate dislike...

This letting 'I would not' wait upon 'I would' produces an effect
which is best seen as ridicule. In this third section, beginning
'Damn with faint praise', the vocabulary of blame is combined
with words that check and modify the anger. So we move, not
into greater and greater anger, but into ridicule and contempt.
The figure of Atticus is belittled. There are words like 'foe'
which blame; there are words like 'tim'rous' which take from
the blame without increasing the praise. A timorous foe is a
nasty thing to have around the place, but not especially dreadful. Looked at like this, the case against Atticus seems to be that
he is a coward. This is no slight criticism of him. In the book of
an eighteenth-century gentleman, only a few sword-thrusts away
from the Civil War, a coward would rank lower even than a villain or a fool. Atticus is worse than a fool; he sits attendant
upon the praise of fools. The 'blame' language, modified into
ridicule, gives rise to the picture of a mock senator. It is blame-
worthy in a Roman senator to court applause, but it is ridiculous
for a man of letters to give himself the airs of a senator. We are
asked (17–21) to contemplate the pretentiousness of an eight-

eenth-century coffee house deliberating solemnly in the manner of a Roman forum. So the comedy rises –

> While Wits and Templars ev'ry sentence raise,
> And wonder with a foolish face of praise; –
> Who but must laugh, if such a man there be?...

Left here, the poem would be a comic portrait, one of many character-sketches that delighted the seventeenth and eighteenth centuries alike. But Pope does not leave the matter here. All along, the metre with its regular stress and regular rhyme has maintained continuity, so that even at the end we are not formally very far from the regulated praise of the beginning. At this point (line 22) Pope forces us to remember that initial praise –

> were there one whose fires
> True genius kindles, and fair Fame inspires;
> . . . .
> Who would not weep if Atticus were he?

If this coffee-house Cato were a mere buffoon, like the scribblers and law-students who surround him, one might laugh. A ridiculous man would then be shown in a posture which invited ridicule. But this is neither wit nor templar; this is a man with the potential of human greatness. It has all been cast away by reason of his pusillanimity. His fall from grace therefore invites, even from the Augustan man-about-town, not comedy but pathos.

The balance of the poem is effected by keeping praise, blame and ridicule in equipoise. If the praise recedes into the background, the judged and certain movement of the verse makes sure it is not lost sight of. Indeed, the justness of the praise is re-established with a fresh poignancy when we realize at length, in that last line, how far the subject of the poem has ceased to deserve it.

In discussing the centre, the language and the tone of the poem, notice that we have also had to discuss its structure. We have shown the way in which one area of meaning gives place to another or contrasts with it. This may well be typified as Praise (lines 1–4); Blame (lines 5–8); Increasing Ridicule (lines 9–21); Praise (line 22). Consideration of structure will be to the fore in our discussion of the next poem, a twentieth-century work by a nineteenth-century master.

DURING WIND AND RAIN

They sing their dearest songs –
He, she, all of them – yea,
Treble and tenor and bass,
    And one to play;
With the candles mooning each face. . . .
    Ah, no; the years O!
How the sick leaves reel down in throngs!

They clear the creeping moss –
Elders and juniors – aye,
Making the pathways neat
    And the garden gay;
And they build a shady seat. . . .
    Ah, no; the years, the years;
See, the white storm-birds wing across!

They are blithely breakfasting all –
Men and maidens – yea,
Under the summer tree,
    With a glimpse of the bay,
While pet fowl come to the knee. . . .
    Ah, no; the years O!
And the rotten rose is ript from the wall.

They change to a high new house,
He, she, all of them – aye,
Clocks and carpets and chairs
    On the lawn all day,
And brightest things that are theirs. . . .
    Ah, no; the years, the years;
Down their carved names the rain-drop ploughs.

THOMAS HARDY

Like many of Hardy's better poems, this piece is more compli-
cated than it looks. It has not one centre but several. Each one
is, however, more emphatically brought out than the last.

> How the sick leaves reel down in throngs...
>
> See, the white storm-birds wing across...
>
> And the rotten rose is ript from the wall...
>
> Down their carved names the rain-drop ploughs...

Notice the concreteness of the language. As I said regarding
other poems, this guarantees the authenticity of the experience
conveyed. The leaves do not just fall; they reel, like sick men
striving to hold themselves on end. The movement mimes the
sense; it is heavy, it lurches.

These climactic lines contrast violently with the light and tripping stanzas of which they are ostensibly part. This contrast is
brought out by the wrenching of the rhythm; I doubt whether
any of the climactic lines, in context, can be scanned. Great
weight is laid on the stresses, and there is a high proportion of
stressed to unstressed syllables.

But, even in this contrast, there is contiguity. This is found not
only in the proximity of each climactic line to its parent stanza,
nor in the fact that each carries a rhyme word, but also in a kind
of calculated mockery of the hopes of man as stated in the main
body of the poem. In the first stanza the family sing their favourite songs, but the last line parodies the basic dance movement; in
more senses than one, it reels. The climactic lines of the next two
stanzas intercross, so that the forlorn storm-birds of stanza two
relate to the pet fowl of stanza three. Similarly, the garden activities of stanza two are transmuted into the decay instinct in the
last line of stanza three –

> And the rotten rose is ript from the wall.

Structurally, then, the poem is an amalgam of two contrasted
works, one about a hopeful family, the other, four lines long,
about the inevitability of death and decay. Each of these works

is broken into four parts, and each single part of the 'hope' poem is contrasted with a part of the four line poem about despair. The effect may be represented in part as Aw/By/Cx/Dz.

Most poignant of all is the contrast in the last stanza. By that time we have become conditioned to expect the worst to happen. The hopes of the family changing to their high new house are mocked even while they are in the process of removal. What the refrain does here is to symbolize their destruction. It makes a connection with the rest of the stanza: the people move to a new house; a house is a thing of walls; walls are stone; stone decays. It equally makes a connection with the other refrain-lines: the rotten rose is ripped from the wall in stanza three, leaving the stone; but in stanza four, even the stone decays. My paraphrase does not do justice to the vigour of Hardy's language; in fact, the raindrop *ploughs* the stone, not to fertilize, but to efface. The lively family whom we have seen singing, gardening, picnicking and moving house are not allowed to remain even as a memory, for

> Down their carved names the rain-drop ploughs.

As well as looking at the centre – centres, in this case – we have broadened our analysis to take in considerations of language, tone and, in looking at these tonal contrasts, structure. Equally, as with the other poems discussed, this is not the only possible approach. The components of a good poem are many and various, and no one account is going to do justice to them all. Criticism, in other words, is not the end of reading a poem; it is the beginning.

Contrast of language, then, indicates contrast of tone; contrast of tone implies a consideration of structure; and, as our discussion of the next poem will show, this can lead to an analysis of dramatic form.

JOURNEY OF THE MAGI

'A cold coming we had of it,
Just the worst time of the year

For a journey, and such a long journey:
The ways deep and the weather sharp,
The very dead of winter.'
And the camels galled, sore-footed, refractory,
Lying down in the melting snow.
There were times we regretted
The summer palaces on slopes, the terraces,
And the silken girls bringing sherbet.
Then the camel men cursing and grumbling
And running away, and wanting their liquor and women,
And the night-fires going out, and the lack of shelters,
And the cities hostile and the towns unfriendly
And the villages dirty and charging high prices:
A hard time we had of it.
At the end we preferred to travel all night,
Sleeping in snatches,
With the voices singing in our ears, saying
That this was all folly.

Then at dawn we came down to a temperate valley,
Wet, below the snow line, smelling of vegetation;
With a running stream and a water-mill beating the darkness,
And three trees on the low sky,
And an old white horse galloped away in the meadow.
Then we came to a tavern with vine-leaves over the lintel,
Six hands at an open door dicing for pieces of silver,
And feet kicking the empty wine-skins.
But there was no information, and so we continued
And arrived at evening, not a moment too soon
Finding the place; it was (you may say) satisfactory.

All this was a long time ago, I remember,
And I would do it again, but set down
This set down
This: were we led all that way for
Birth or Death? There was a Birth, certainly,
We had evidence and no doubt. I had seen birth and death,
But had thought they were different; this Birth was
Hard and bitter agony for us, like Death, our death.

We returned to our places, these Kingdoms,
But no longer at ease here, in the old dispensation,
With an alien people clutching their gods.
I should be glad of another death.

                                                                    T. S. ELIOT

The centre here is at the beginning! We are confronted with
the fact of a hard journey. It is acted out in touches of sharp
detail – 'the camels ... lying down in the melting snow ... a
temperate valley, wet, below the snow line ... three trees on the
low sky ...' But the detail exists on at least two levels. This is not
just the description of one particular journey but a symbolic pattern referring to others. The three trees irresistibly remind us of
the three crosses on which Jesus and the robbers hung. Even
though the Kings are called to the Nativity, it is the Crucifixion
that is suggested –

     Six hands at an open door dicing for pieces of silver.

This conflates the silver paid to Judas with the soldiers dicing for
Christ's garments. It is detail like this, at once descriptive and
symbolic, that reinforces the puzzlement behind the speaker's
question –

          were we led all that way for
          Birth or Death?

We are brought to the recognition that the hard journey of the
poem is itself symbolic. It represents, among other things, the
difficult path the Christian takes after conversion. After they have
been present at the Nativity, the Kings are

     no longer at ease here, in the old dispensation.

The whole poem is a feat of encapsulation. We have the tone of
a Magus speaking, the weary tone of a man who has suffered to
the extreme of his endurance. There is a shudder in the speeding
up of the rhythm towards the end of the first line; distaste in the
heavy emphasis upon the words 'worst' and 'journey'; a sense of
muscular effort, of kinaesthesia, in the consonantally end-

stopped words 'deep', 'sharp', 'dead'. This would seem to put the poem sharply in the present. Yet it records a journey that must have taken many months; it retells the Nativity story; it forecasts the Crucifixion; it intimates the agonies of the life to come. Moreover, the poem cannot really be in the present, for it is spoken by a Magus, and such a figure, if he had said anything, would have said it two thousand years ago. The form is that of the dramatic monologue, and it is ironic that it should be Eliot, usually considered a difficult 'modern', whose work should be the only poem here capable of being so readily placed in a category. The dramatic monologue can be taken as a poem spoken by someone other than the author; that embodies some revelation of character; that conveys the feel and presence of a dramatic situation. As this will suggest, a dramatic monologue is a concise substitute for a play. It is as though this speech occurred in Act V of an otherwise unwritten drama. One should make a distinction, however: the speech conveys the essence of that part of the drama not played out before. It is couched in a form that is an excellent way of handling experience economically. Eliot gets through a great deal in comparatively few lines. That, in itself, would not make the poem a success. But we should consider the immediate scenic effect of the journey, the way in which the larger issues of crucifixion and conversion are implied, and, not least, the way in which the tone of the poem conveys the voice and character of the Magus. When this is brought under review, we see that Eliot is a direct and living poet, in many respects not unlike Herbert (whom he greatly admired) and Hardy.

There are, of course, obvious differences between the poems under discussion. For one thing, each of the authors grew up in a different century. 'They flee from me' was written in the 1520s and 'The Journey of the Magi' in the 1920s. One would certainly expect some difference of technique in a period covering four hundred years. But we have seen that these poems, different as they are, do not require wildly different approaches. Moreover, each particular approach implies something of another. It is impossible to discuss what I have called the centre without bringing in the question of appropriateness in language. When we discuss language, we necessarily bring in our reactions to the tone of a poem – how it would condition, in delivery, an ideal speaking voice. Tone relates to form the moment we begin to compare disparate areas of language with each other within the total structure of the poem. In the end, it does not matter where we start with a poem, so long as what we bring into consideration is relevant to the text under discussion. That is to say, if we look at the poem and do not substitute for it fantasy, biography, point-scoring or the like, we shall find ourselves bringing some part of our reaction into rationality and conveying it to other readers.

The rational discourse cannot replace the poem. But you may help others, as well as yourself, if you make clear what you understand of your reading. At the best, critical analysis allows us to make sure that a text has been looked at as carefully as is practicable. In any case, such analysis is a way of developing one's powers of reasoned discussion.

III Four modes of fiction

There are almost as many ways of reading fiction as there are readers. However, some modes of writing assert themselves more strongly than others. This is especially true if we read the classics: those texts which have lasted beyond their immediate period and survive into our own.

Some novels signal to us in such a way as to create the anticipation of comedy. They have a kind of realism that is restrained or angled so as to preclude our identifying with the central character; the protagonist. This entails the notation of character and events in a manner explicit enough to render them recognizable. However, it does not entail photographic naturalism. We can adopt a term patented by Northrop Frye and call this mode *Low-Mimetic*. Professor Frye used this term as a way of describing protagonists who fail to rise above their environment. Here I adapt it to suggest a kind of writing which is narrative without being intensely dramatic.

If there is a low-mimetic mode, it would be logical to infer that there must be a high-mimetic mode as well. This may be identified with tragedy, where the language acts out the meaning in a highly dramatic way. In prose, it is what F. R. Leavis called 'The Novel as Dramatic Poem'. One need not altogether empathize with the protagonist; but one tends to, in the *High-Mimetic* mode.

Sometimes, however, we may be conscious of a distance deliberately imposed between us and the characters. They are held up for our amused contemplation, often to the accompaniment of a good deal of authorial comment. Sometimes, indeed, the author himself is a palpable presence, a stage-manager or puppet-master, quite explicitly telling us what to think. This mode is sometimes ironic, sometimes moralistic. Quite often we are aware of a split level of narration: the author may separate the foolish character's point of view from his own informed one in order to satirize what he considers to be ridiculous behaviour or to point a moral. This is what may be termed the *Didactic* mode.

A mode which has been particularly wide-spread among serious authors in the twentieth century attempts realism through imitating the consciousness of particular characters. This mode has predecessors in the eighteenth century: when a character in *Tristram Shandy* by Laurence Sterne becomes unconscious, the page goes black! Nowadays, writing that follows the protagonists' consciousness tends to be associated with two spectacular exponents of this mode, James Joyce and Virginia Woolf. One cannot, without many qualifications, term them realistic, for the flicker of attention is necessarily stylized when given a degree of permanence in fictional form. When bits of detail are seen to be dispersed in such a way as to simulate an intermittent consciousness, the mode may be termed *Impressionist*.

One of the best exponents of the first of these modes, the Low-Mimetic, is Jane Austen.

From: *Pride and Prejudice* (1813) Volume I, Chapter iii

Elizabeth Bennet had been obliged, by the scarcity of gentlemen, to sit down for two dances; and during part of that time, Mr Darcy had been standing near enough for her to overhear a conversation between him and Mr Bingley, who came from the dance for a few minutes to press his friend to join it.

'Come, Darcy,' said he, 'I must have you dance. I hate to see you standing about by yourself in this stupid manner. You had much better dance.'

'I certainly shall not. You know how I detest it, unless I am particularly acquainted with my partner. At such an assembly as this, it would be insupportable. Your sisters are engaged, and there is not another woman in the room whom it would not be a punishment to me to stand up with.'

'I would not be so fastidious as you are,' cried Bingley, 'for a kingdom! Upon my honour, I never met with so many pleasant girls in my life as I have this evening; and there are several of them, you see, uncommonly pretty.'

'*You* are dancing with the only handsome girl in the room,' said Mr Darcy, looking at the eldest Miss Bennet.

'Oh, she is the most beautiful creature I ever beheld! But there is one of her sisters sitting down just behind you, who is very pretty, and I daresay very agreeable. Do let me ask my partner to introduce you.'

'Which do you mean?' and turning round, he looked for a moment at Elizabeth, till, catching her eye, he withdrew his own, and coldly said, 'She is tolerable, but not handsome enough to tempt *me;* and I am in no humour at present to give consequence to young ladies who are slighted by other men. You had better return to your partner and enjoy her smiles, for you are wasting your time with me.'

Mr Bingley followed his advice. Mr Darcy walked off; and Elizabeth remained with no very cordial feelings towards him. She told the story, however, with great spirit among her friends; for she had a lively, playful disposition, which delighted in anything ridiculous.

JANE AUSTEN

We are given an insight into Elizabeth's feelings but we are not encouraged to identify with her. In close proximity to this insight there is a comment on Elizabeth – 'lively, playful' – which could come only from the author. The centre of consciousness in *Pride and Prejudice* relates to the way in which its protagonist sees things, but it includes more detachment and perception than she as yet possesses. We never lose the sense that the book is an account of a young woman growing out of prejudice and into judgement. Necessarily, there is an element of distance in the comedy. Darcy's behaviour causes Elizabeth some indignation, but it is not relayed to us directly in her voice. The novel is written in a third person: there is an intermediary that sees what Elizabeth sees, and more besides. In other words, the narrative is refracted in such a way as to inhibit dramatic confrontation. Nothing is taken to extremes.

Jane Austen did not invent this mode. She learned a good deal from her predecessors, including some who may be seen as less talented than herself. To say that a piece of writing is in a given mode is not necessarily to imply an evaluation. It is plain that the ball scene in *Pride and Prejudice* derives from a similar scene in an earlier novel; but it is obvious that this novel is a cruder performance altogether.

From: *Evelina* (1778), Letter XII

It must have passed while I was sitting with Mrs Mirvan in the card-room. Maria was taking some refreshment, and saw Lord Orville advancing for the same purpose himself; but he did not know her, though she immediately recollected him. Presently after, a very gay-looking man, stepping hastily up to him, cried, 'Why, my Lord, what have you done with your lovely partner?'

'*Nothing!*' answered Lord Orville with a smile and a shrug.

'By Jove,' cried the man, 'she is the most beautiful creature I ever saw in my life!'

Lord Orville, as he well might, laughed; but answered, 'Yes, a pretty modest-looking girl.'

'O my Lord!' cried the madman, 'she is an angel!'

'A *silent* one,' returned he.

'Why ay, my Lord, how stands she as to that? She looks all intelligence and expression.'

'A poor weak girl!' answered Lord Orville, shaking his head.

'By Jove,' cried the other, 'I am glad to hear it!'

At that moment, the same odious creature who had been my former tormentor, joined them. Addressing Lord Orville with great respect, he said, 'I beg pardon, my Lord, – if I was – as I fear might be the case – rather too severe in my censure of the lady who is honoured with your protection – but, my Lord, ill-breeding is apt to provoke a man.'

'Ill-breeding!' cried my unknown champion, 'impossible! that elegant face can never be so vile a mask!'

'O Sir, as to that,' answered he, 'you must allow *me* to judge; for though I pay all deference to your opinion – in other things, – yet

I hope you will grant – and I appeal to your Lordship also – that I am not totally despicable as a judge of good or ill-manners.'

'I was so wholly ignorant,' said Lord Orville, gravely, 'of the provocation you might have had, that I could not but be surprised at your singular resentment.'

'It was far from my intention', answered he, 'to offend your lordship; but, really, for a person who is nobody, to give herself such airs, – I own I could not command my passion. For, my Lord, though I have made diligent inquiry – I cannot learn who she is.'

'By what I can make out,' cried my defender, 'she must be a country parson's daughter.'

'He! he! he! very good, 'pon honour!' cried the fop; – 'well, so I could have sworn by her manners.'

And then, delighted at his own wit, he laughed, and went away, as I suppose, to repeat it.

FANNY BURNEY

As in *Pride and Prejudice,* the scene is described partly through the eyes of the young woman who is the protagonist of the novel. 'It [the ensuing dialogue] must have passed while I was sitting with Mrs Mirvan in the card-room.' Unlike *Pride and Prejudice,* however, this novel is written largely in the first person, mostly in the form of letters from Evelina to her guardian and friends. But this circumstance does not prevent our having a sense of the author's implied presence. Nothing in this passage, or indeed in the book itself, would lead us to believe the passive Evelina capable of the sarcasm of the last line quoted: 'And then, delighted at his own wit, he laughed, and went away, as I suppose, to repeat it.' This is not the 'silent angel' talking but a lively and informed narrator. Since the book is very much about Evelina, the third-person narrative in this case brings about an instability of mode. The problem of reconciling third-person perceptions with first-person narrative is more satisfactorily solved in the following.

From: *Clarissa* (1747–48) Letter XVII

Before the usual breakfast-time was over my father withdrew with my mother, telling her he wanted to speak to her. Then my sister and next my aunt (who was with us) dropped away.

My brother gave himself some airs of insult, which I understood well enough; but which Mr Solmes could make nothing of: and at last he arose from *his* seat. Sister, said he, I have a curiosity to show you. I will fetch it. And away he went; shutting the door close after him.

I saw what all this was for. I arose; the man hemming up for a speech, rising and beginning to set his splay feet [indeed, my dear, the man in all his ways is hateful to me!] in an approaching posture. I will save my brother the trouble of bringing to me his curiosity, said I. I curtsied – your servant, sir. The man cried, madam, madam, twice, and looked like a fool. But away I went – to find my brother to save my word. But my brother, indifferent as the weather was, was gone to walk in the garden with my sister. A plain case that he had left his *curiosity* with me, and designed to show me no other.

SAMUEL RICHARDSON

More evidently than the writing of Jane Austen or Fanny Burney, this is dramatic. The passage is seen through the eyes of the young woman concerned, but the distance varies. The first sentence shows us the figure at a remove, but, by the second paragraph, we are much nearer. At this point the prose breaks down, quite appropriately considering the subject, into dialogue. The family is making itself scarce in order to give the suitor free play. When the brother leaves, Mr Solmes is uncomfortably near – through Clarissa's eyes, we notice his splay feet. The narrative varies in distance all the time. Sometimes the prose resembles in its curtness and precision the mode adopted by stage directions, and the dialogue incorporates an effect of interruption normally associated with the theatre. Indeed, there were certain playwrights whom we know Richardson to have liked. They will be found, however, to lack his subtlety.

From: *The London Merchant* (1731)

To her BARNWELL, *bowing very low.* LUCY *at a distance.*
Millwood. Sir! the surprise and joy –
Barnwell. Madam –

Millwood. This is such a favour.   *Advancing*
Barnwell. Pardon me, madam.
Millwood. So unhoped for.   *Still advances*

GEORGE LILLO

Richardson has the advantage over the old dramatists of being able to get inside his characters. We never lose sight in his narrative mode of the consciousness of the central figures. Like other novels of the period, *Clarissa* is told in letters. But, in the hands of Richardson, this means that we have a number of possible viewpoints clearly diversified. Despite this, we are never in doubt of the narrative framework. Description does not swamp the reader; neither does it evaporate and leave the dialogue devoid of authorial judgement.

Richardson has been called, by Mark Kinkead-Weekes, the Shakespeare of Prose! Only Shakespeare can be called that, unless some readers feel the title should go to Dickens in order to acknowledge that, like Richardson, Dickens got some of his best effects from the theatre. He adapted them, however, into a very different mode.

From: *Bleak House* (1852—3) Chapter XXXII

... Mr Guppy sitting on the window-sill, nodding his head and balancing all these possibilities in his mind, continues thoughtfully to tap it, and clasp it, and measure it with his hand, until he hastily draws his hand away.

'What, in the Devil's name,' he says, 'is this! Look at my fingers!'

A thick, yellow liquor defiles them, which is offensive to the touch and sight, and more offensive to the smell. A stagnant, sickening oil, with some natural repulsion in it that makes them both shudder.

'What have you been doing here? What have you been pouring out of window?'

'I pouring out of window! Nothing, I swear! Never, since I have been here!' cries the lodger.

And yet look here – and look here! When he brings the candle, here, from the corner of the window-sill, it slowly drips and creeps away down the bricks; here, lies in a little thick nauseous pool.

'This is a horrible house', says Mr Guppy, shutting down the window. 'Give me some water, or I shall cut my hand off.'

He so washes, and rubs, and scrubs, and smells, and washes, that he has not long restored himself with a glass of brandy, and stood silently before the fire, when Saint Paul's bell strikes twelve, and all those other bells strike twelve from their towers of various heights in the dark air, and in their many tones. When all is quiet again, the lodger says:

'It's the appointed time at last. Shall I go?'

Mr Guppy nods, and gives him a 'lucky touch' on the back; but not with the washed hand, though it is his right hand.

He goes downstairs; and Mr Guppy tries to compose himself, before the fire, for waiting a long time. But in no more than a minute or two the stairs creak, and Tony comes swiftly back.

'Have you got them?'

'Got them! No. The old man's not there.'

He has been so horribly frightened in the short interval, that his terror seizes the other, who makes a rush at him, and asks loudly, 'What's the matter?'

'I couldn't make him hear, and I softly opened the door and looked in. And the burning smell is there – and the soot is there, and the oil is there – and he is not there!' – Tony ends this with a groan.

Mr Guppy takes the light. They go down, more dead than alive, and holding one another, push open the door of the back shop. The cat has retreated close to it, and stands snarling – not at them; at something on the ground, before the fire. There is very little fire left in the grate, but there is a smouldering suffocating vapour in the room, and a dark greasy coating on the walls and ceiling. The chairs and table, and the bottle so rarely absent from the table all stand as usual. On one chair-back, hang the old man's hairy cap and coat...

...'What's the matter with the cat?' says Mr Guppy. 'Look at her!'

'Mad, I think. And no wonder, in this evil place.'

They advance slowly, looking at all these things. The cat remains where they found her, still snarling at the something on the ground, before the fire and between the two chairs. What is it? Hold up the light.

Here is a small burnt patch of flooring; here is the tinder from a little bundle of burnt paper, but not so light as usual, seeming to be steeped in something; and here is – is it the cinder of a small charred and broken log of wood sprinkled with white ashes, or is it coal? O Horror, he is here! and this, from which we run away, striking out the light and overturning one another into the street, is all that represents him.

CHARLES DICKENS

This is the High-Mimetic mode *par excellence*. The prose seems impersonal in one sense of the word, yet it brings its significant details almost under our noses. We are, for the moment, quite close to the character, Guppy. The closeness lies in the immediacy of the writing: it accumulates sensations. There is touch: 'he hastily draws his hand away', '"look at my fingers!"', 'a thick, yellow liquor defiles them'. There is hearing: 'Saint Paul's bell strikes twelve', in sonorous monosyllables. There is smell: 'a smouldering suffocating vapour in the room'. In however uncertain a light, we can see; but what we see is horrific: 'a small charred and broken log of wood sprinkled with white ashes'. This, we understand almost immediately, is all that is left of Old Krook, the rag-and-bone merchant. He has blown himself up by ingesting spirituous liquors. The fact that this could not happen in real life does not diminish its effect here. Nevertheless, one could not imagine any of this in Jane Austen!

The dialogue, like the sensory effect, is thrust upon us –

'What have you been doing here? What have you been pouring out of window?'
'I pouring out of window! Nothing, I swear! Never, since I have been here!'

The rhythm in both description and dialogue is strongly marked. One could almost scan Dickens as verse. He writes here in a mode stemming not from the bourgeois theatre of George Lillo so much as from poetic drama; perhaps, especially, Shakespearian tragedy at its most emotionally fraught.

From: *Macbeth* (1606) Act II

Macbeth.	I have done the deed. Didst thou not hear a noise?
Lady Macbeth.	I heard the owl scream and the crickets cry. Did not you speak?
Macbeth.	When?
Lady Macbeth.	Now.
Macbeth.	As I descended?
Lady Macbeth.	Ay.
Macbeth.	Hark! Who lies i' the second chamber?
Lady Macbeth.	Donalbain.
Macbeth.	This is a sorry sight. *[Looking on his hands]*
Lady Macbeth.	A foolish thought, to say a sorry sight.
Macbeth.	There's one did laugh in's sleep, and one cried 'Murder!' That they did wake each other: I stood and heard them: But they did say their prayers, and address'd them Again to sleep.
Lady Macbeth.	There are two lodg'd together.
Macbeth.	One cried 'God bless us!' and 'Amen' the other, As they had seen me with these hangman's hands: Listening their fear, I could not say 'Amen,' When they did say 'God bless us!'
Lady Macbeth.	Consider it not so deeply.
Macbeth.	But wherefore could not I pronounce 'Amen'? I had most need of blessing, and 'Amen' Stuck in my throat.

WILLIAM SHAKESPEARE

Both Shakespeare and Dickens rely on thrusting sharp details upon our attention. In Dickens, some of these details occur as description and others occur in the dialogue. In Shakespeare, all is dialogue. In this example, it is terse, miming the emotion of the speakers. However, the dialogue may very well contain description –

> Will all great Neptune's ocean wash this blood
> Clean from my hand...?

The High-Mimetic mode, moreover, can go higher than this. Sometimes, for effect, Shakespeare practically lifts the language on to stilts. Occasionally this is to show dissimulation –

> Here lay Duncan,
> His silver skin lac'd with his golden blood...

Sometimes the language is raised to show mania, as with the grandiloquent Antony, in *Antony and Cleopatra* –

> Where souls do couch on flowers, we'll hand in hand,
> And with our sprightly port make the ghosts gaze...

The High-Mimetic mode can get even higher, but it seldom works at such an altitude, and especially not in prose. Consider this –

Ah! wretched men, what woe is this ye suffer? Shrouded in night are your heads and faces and knees, and kindled is the voice of wailing, and all cheeks are wet with tears, and the walls and the fair spaces between the pillars are sprinkled with blood...

or this –

Far and gray, on the heath, the dreadful strides of ghosts are seen: the ghosts of those who fell bend forward to their song. Bid, O Cathmor! the harps to rise, to brighten the dead, on their wandering blasts...

These are, respectively, the Butcher and Lang (1879) translation of Homer's *Odyssey* and James Macpherson's entirely spurious 'translation' (1763) of the Gaelic bard, Ossian. In verse such writing might be termed the Grand Style; but, even in verse, it often fails. In prose, the reader is liable to be embarrassed by the over-statement – 'wretched men, what woe' – and bludgeoning emphasis – 'dreadful strides of ghosts'. This is the High-Mimetic mode gone wrong. Fortunately, it is a kind of writing we hardly ever come across now. One can see from all this that value resides not in the mode itself but in the way in which the author handles it. Shakespeare can use as a special effect what for Butcher and Lang and for Macpherson is mere posturing, empty of emotional content.

Almost at the other extreme is the mode which may be termed Didactic. It is one where the author is very definitely present and where, therefore, everything else is liable to seem somewhat diminished. Certainly the descriptive details in the following passage seem at a considerable distance from the reader.

From: *Pendennis* (1848–53) Chapter I

At sunset, from the lawn of Fairoaks, there was a pretty sight; it and the opposite park of Clavering were in the habit of putting on a rich golden tinge, which became them both wonderfully. The upper windows of the great house flamed so as to make your eyes wink; the little river ran off noisily westward, and was lost in a sombre wood, behind which the towers of the old abbey church of Clavering (whereby that town is called Clavering St Mary's to the present day) rose up in purple splendour. Little Arthur's figure and his mother's cast long blue shadows over the grass: and he would repeat in a low voice (for a scene of great natural beauty always moved the boy, who inherited this sensibility from his mother) certain lines beginning, 'These are Thy glorious works, Parent of God; Almighty! Thine this universal frame,' greatly to Mrs Pendennis's delight. Such walks and conversations generally ended in a profusion of filial and maternal embraces: for to love and to pray were the main occupations of this dear woman's life: and I have often heard Pendennis say in his wild way, that he felt that he was sure of going to heaven, for his mother never could be happy there without him.

W. M. Thackeray

The nineteenth-century reader was more attuned to this mode than is his counterpart in the twentieth century. In those days the literate minority had a good deal of leisure and often required not only to be amused but also instructed. Thackeray here assumes what has been called the role of the omniscient narrator. That is to say, he observes, on our behalf, the sunset, the lawn, the house; he overhears the boy reciting to his mother, claims his acquaintance after he has grown up, and makes explicit comments on the action as it proceeds. We are not allowed to identify with the characters. The author is plainly distinguishable in his plot; directing, stage-managing, even prompting. Thackeray himself, at the end of his most famous novel, *Vanity Fair,* compared his activity with that of a puppet-master. It is at an extreme from the High-Mimetic mode of narration favoured by his great rival, Dickens. Though it shares some attributes with the Low-Mimetic mode, it differs in placing much more weight upon the explicit presence of the narrator.

Like the Low-Mimetic mode – that of Jane Austen, for example – the Didactic mode has its roots in the eighteenth century. In this particular case, the opening of *Pendennis,* it most obviously derives from Henry Fielding.

From: *Tom Jones* (1749) Book I Chapter 2

In that part of the western division of this kingdom which is commonly called Somersetshire, there lately lived and perhaps lives still, a gentleman whose name was Allworthy, and who might well be called the favourite of both Nature and Fortune; for both of these seem to have contended which should bless and enrich him most. In this contention Nature may seem to some to have come off victorious, as she bestowed on him many gifts, while Fortune had only one gift in her power; but in pouring forth this, she was so very profuse, that others perhaps may think this single endowment to have been more than equivalent to all the various blessings which he enjoyed from Nature. From the former of these he derived an agreeable person, a sound constitution, a sane understanding, and a benevolent heart; by the latter, he was decreed to the inheritance of one of the largest estates in the county.

This gentleman had in his youth married a very worthy and beautiful woman, of whom he had been extremely fond: by her he had three children, all of whom died in their infancy. He had likewise had the misfortune of burying his beloved wife herself, about five years before the time in which this history chooses to set out. This loss, however great, he bore like a man of sense and constancy, though it must be confessed he would often talk a little whimsically on this head; for he sometimes said he looked on himself as still married, and considered his wife as only gone a little before him, a journey which he should most certainly, sooner or later, take after her; and that he had not the least doubt of meeting her again in a place where he should never part with her more – sentiments for which his sense was arraigned by one part of his neighbours, his religion by a second, and his sincerity by a third.

HENRY FIELDING

We note the expansive manner, the leisured delivery, the air of knowing past as well as present events; knowing, also, not only the central characters but the context that surrounds them. In its turn, the mode derives from the essays and character sketches of the seventeenth and eighteenth centuries, which are best considered as a secular and genial form of sermonizing – 'He is now in his fifty-sixth year, cheerful, gay, and hearty; keeps a good house both in town and country; a great lover of mankind; but there is such a mirthful cast in his behaviour, that he is rather beloved than esteemed'. That is the fictional Sir Roger de Coverley, described on his first entry into *The Spectator* (1711–14), a periodical written almost entirely by two authors, Joseph Addison and Richard Steele.

In the twentieth century – certainly until the 1950s – the sophisticated reader tended to expect something very different in fiction; the Impressionist mode. This contrasts very strongly with the Didactic mode, which was not much favoured during this period, and relates to the High-Mimetic mode in so far as that mode derives from drama. The difference between the High-Mimetic mode and Impressionism is that the latter tends to break up a dramatic narrative very much after the manner in which the individual characters might be thought to have experienced it.

From: *Jacob's Room* (1922) Chapter 1

'So of course,' wrote Betty Flanders, pressing her heels rather deeper in the sand, 'there was nothing for it but to leave.'

Slowly welling from the point of her gold nib, pale blue ink dissolved the full stop; for there her pen stuck; her eyes fixed, and tears slowly filled them. The entire bay quivered; the lighthouse wobbled; and she had the illusion that the mast of Mr Connor's little yacht was bending like a wax candle in the sun. She winked quickly. Accidents were awful things. She winked again. The mast was straight; the waves were regular; the lighthouse was upright; but the blot had spread.

'...nothing for it but to leave,' she read.

'Well, if Jacob doesn't want to play' (the shadow of Archer, her eldest son, fell across the notepaper and looked blue on the sand, and she felt chilly – it was the third of September already), 'if Jacob doesn't want to play' – what a horrid blot! It must be getting late.

VIRGINIA WOOLF

When Betty Flanders cries, the bay quivers and the lighthouse wobbles. In other words, the tears in her eyes distort the landscape. This is because the landscape exists as something seen by her; it is the product of her vision. Though this seems modern in its approach, John Donne in the early seventeenth century addressed the sun, saying 'I could eclipse and cloud thee with a wink'. Bishop Berkeley wrote in the eighteenth century that things only existed in the minds of those perceiving them. However, there can be no doubt that highly personalized viewpoints such as these are more widespread in the twentieth century than in centuries preceding. One of the greatest exponents of impressionism was an exact contemporary of Virginia Woolf, writing quite independently of her.

From: *Ulysses* (1922) Proteus

A bloated carcass of a dog lay lolled on bladderwrack. Before him the gunwale of a boat, sunk in sand. *Un coche ensablé,* Louis Veuillot

called Gautier's prose. These heavy sands are language tide and wind
have silted here. And there, the stoneheaps of dead builders, a warren
of weasel rats. Hide gold there. Try it. You have some. Sands and
stones. Heavy of the past. Sir Lout's toys. Mind you don't get one
bang on the ear. I'm the bloody well gigant rolls all them bloody well
boulders, bones for my steppingstones. Feefawfum. I zmellz de bloodz
odz an Iridzman.

JAMES JOYCE

Notice that the description is broken up into sense-impres-
sions and is interspersed with the random thoughts of the narrator who is the protagonist. This protagonist is Stephen Dedalus,
a young man walking on the strand. The stream of consciousness, as this form of writing is called, can go even further. James
Joyce himself went on to write a book, *Finnegans Wake* (1939),
in which a sleeping man half-remembers, half-fantasizes, jour-
neys and events – 'Eins within a space and a weary wide space it
was ere wohned a Mookse.'

I have already instanced Donne and Berkeley as being rather
isolated examples of the Impressionist mode in their own time.
More accessible and definitely more popular in his own period,
which was just before the onset of Romanticism, was Laurence
Sterne.

From: Tristram Shandy (1759–65) Book IV

Chapter XI

We shall bring all things to rights, said my father, setting his foot upon
the first step from the landing. – This Trismegistus, continued my
father, drawing his leg back and turning to my uncle Toby – was the
greatest (Toby) of all earthly beings – he was the greatest king – the
greatest law-giver – the greatest philosopher – and the greatest priest
– and engineer – said my uncle Toby.

– In course, said my father.

Chapter XII

– And how does your mistress? cried my father, taking the same step over again from the landing, and calling to Susannah, whom he saw passing by the foot of the stairs with a huge pin-cushion in her hand – how does your mistress? As well, said Susannah, tripping by, but without looking up, as can be expected. – What a fool am I! said my father, drawing his leg back again – let things be as they will, brother Toby, 'tis ever the precise answer – And how is the child, pray? – No answer. And where is Dr Slop? added my father, raising his voice aloud, and looking over the ballusters – Susannah was out of hearing.

Of all the riddles of a married life, said my father, crossing the landing in order to set his back against the wall, whilst he propounded it to my uncle Toby – of all the puzzling riddles, said he, in a marriage state, – of which you may trust me, brother Toby, there are more asses loads than all Job's stock of asses could have carried – there is not one that has more intricacies in it than this – that from the very moment the mistress of the house is brought to bed, every female in it, from my lady's gentlewoman down to the cinder-wench, becomes an inch taller for it; and give themselves more airs upon that single inch, than all their other inches put together.

LAURENCE STERNE

Here we are supposed to be aware that the consciousness is that of the narrator who is also the hero of the book. Everybody exists in so far as they relate to him, and yet he does not succeed in getting born until the third section of his narrative. What we experience ourselves in reading the book is a mixture of hearsay and recollection, all told in a form of realism that is vivid but broken. Such fragmentation makes for what was a pioneer stream of consciousness based on the association of ideas. Here, for instance, Mr Shandy's meditations upon the occult philosopher, Hermes Trismegistus, are interrupted by the accident of a maidservant passing, and this brings to his mind the fact that, at this moment, his son has just been born. Though his meditations go on, they do not return to Hermes Trismegistus.

It may be thought that we have looked at variegated modes

here, yet none of our expectations of narrative need be exclusive. There is an element of the Didactic even in Impressionism. In *Tristram Shandy,* for example, the author appears from time to time, and not merely in his role as protagonist, to implore the reader's aid – 'Holla! – you, chairman! – here's sixpence – do step into that bookseller's shop, and call me a *day-tall* critick'. This follows in the chapter following those from which I quoted just now. Even so, Sterne is not didactic as Fielding and Thackeray are. The author is not a puppet-master but a character in the book, though rather a special one, and no explicit moral is put across.

As we have seen, it is possible to write well or badly in any particular mode. But it is our job to read in such a way as to make sense of the text. Quite often our judgement may be impaired by expecting one set of effects from a given mode when in fact another is proffered. There is no point in requiring violent action of Jane Austen; we must look for what she gives us and try to understand it. Similarly, every mode has its economies. To anticipate ironic detachment in Dickens is to ignore the circumstance that this would be incompatible with what in fact he is able to give us: a powerful sense of drama. This is what elsewhere, in my book *A Theory of Communication,* I have called the Principle of the Roving Criterion. One should, figuratively speaking, turn the text about to find the mode of reading that gives the clearest sense of pattern and the clearest pattern in the sense.

IV English prose style

This is a chapter on conceptual prose; that is to say, the prose of non-fiction. It is an astonishing fact that this is the medium we mostly read and through which we mainly express ourselves, and yet for some reason it is the most neglected branch of literature as taught at universities.

I have deliberately drawn the examples that follow chiefly from literary criticism. This is to further two ends. One is to indicate that criticism itself is a form of writing; the other is to show that different modes are possible in argumentative expression. I hope to suggest to you some of the possibilities inherent in the craft of writing a critical essay.

As with the novel, four modes seem to offer the predominant possibilities. There is a mode which hovers round about a text; which, to some extent, seeks to replace it. This is the mode of the literary journalist, the fine writer, the Belletrist.

Another mode became very dominant in the nineteenth century and is especially associated with Victorian hortatory writings. It still persists, though normally only in moments of afflatus or with personages who feel themselves to be isolated in their opinions. It is the mode of the Prophet.

A further mode, attractive to read and difficult to compose, can be read as literature in its own right. We find it characteristically when the critic is very much at home with his text and – sometimes as a result of this – markedly hostile to other critics. He will tend to recommend the text in such a way as to hold alternative interpretations up to contemplation in a register ranging from gentle wit to black sarcasm. This is the mode of the Ironist.

However, there is another approach still. The critic who has great confidence in his material, argument as well as text, tends to rely on that material to get him through. This is not necessarily a simple matter. Many a sustained passage that finally reads persuasively has previously been set up in a number of different ways. The distinguished economist, J. K. Galbraith, said that, in his own writings, he never managed a note of spontaneity until the fifth or sixth draft! I am referring here to a mode that seeks to achieve prose like a pane of clear glass, through which the reader thinks he sees with no refraction the material to be conveyed. I call it the mode of the Expositor.

I am bound to say that these modes may not seem of equal utility to the literary student, especially when he comes to writing essays himself. The mode of the Belletrist has its charms for some, but my feeling is that it tends to dazzle where it should illuminate. For example, here is an extract from an article on the novelist, William Golding.

To read Golding entire, seeking, as it were, to possess him, is to become aware, as may be with any writer, of an *oeuvre* with its own structure of consiliences and reverberations. It is also to experience, in the curving of one man's mind and art, literature as process rather than as product. The individual books, of course, hold to their own lines, but they also melt into each other and in the melting we see development. Accompanying our awareness of the structured body of work is a sense of its inner motions, the processes of its overall metabolism. The processes observable in the work of Golding are of particular interest. For Golding begins with a kind of total assurance, compassionate but rigid, and moves with a momentum that each novel increases, away from the grand, categorised, tightly sealed certainties of *Lord of the Flies,* through *Free Fall*'s Doctor Halde who 'does not know about peoples' and Dean Jocelin's transcendent acquiescence in complexity, to the delicate, unforced recognitions of *The Pyramid.*

If we take the first sentence alone, we may be puzzled at the apparent antithesis between 'consiliences' and 'reverberations'. A consilience is a coming together of lines of reasoning derived from different areas; a reverberation is a repeated or re-echoed sound. The mock-precision of this prose may be seen to be nugatory, however, when we notice that the critic here suggests the structure peculiar to Golding may be held to be so with any writer. Any writer's body of work, in other words, possesses 'its own structure of consiliences and reverberations'. What the critic here is saying is that any *oeuvre* has its own qualities. This is a truism not made any the less truistic by being stated in a pretentious and elaborate manner.

Antithesis is to this critic a habit of style rather than a method of reasoning. What, for example, is the difference between literature as process and literature as product? What is the distinction between the 'certainties' of *Lord of the Flies* and the 'recognitions' of *The Pyramid?* If there really is a difference, it can be brought out only by frequentation and analysis of the text. It certainly cannot be brought out in assertions such as these.

The tendency of the Belletrist mode is to refract its material. If you are unduly aware of the critic's prose, it is quite likely that his prose is over-assertive. But there is no doubt that quite a number of critics tend in this direction. I have no shortage of examples, I assure you.

The basic and constant impulses of the novel always have been toward the panoramic or the intimate or a combination of both. The panoramic inevitably has an affinity with chronicle and, through history, naturally or presumptuously, to the collective extension of epic and myth. The intimate is invariably drawn to introspection and through psychology, humbly or desperately, to the mythic centrality of singular sensibility. The panoramic and the intimate are not accidental or occasional allies subdued to novelistic purposes. Rather their quests for collective or singular definition have about them the character of a novel. The reason history is a natural ally of the novel is that both are unfinished.

If you feel confused by this, do not worry. The confusion is
not in your mind but in the writing. Again we have – what is
highly characteristic of the Belletrist – the false antithesis. In this
case, it is the contrast between the 'panoramic' and the 'intimate'. But the antithesis cannot be as strong as that. In the sentence where the panoramic and the intimate are contrasted, the
critic tells us that they can also be combined. He then goes on to
contradict himself by suggesting that the two impulses belong to
different forms of writing: epic, on the one hand; introspection,
on the other. The critic in question may or may not have a valid
distinction here. All I can say is that the style in which this is
couched serves only to blur it.

Such writing has a history and has attracted considerable
praise. Perhaps its prime exponent was Charles Lamb, who for
almost a century was taken as a guide to essay-writing. In the
example from his work that follows, Lamb appears to be talking
about imaginative painting of the past and the extent to which
the moderns have fallen away from it. But is attention focused
upon any particular work of art or is it not rather drawn to the
ingenious methods the critic finds to talk about Art at large?

From: 'Barrenness of the Imaginative Faculty
in the Productions of Modern Art' (1833)

Hogarth excepted, can we produce any one painter within the last fifty
years, or since the humour of exhibiting began, that has treated a story
imaginatively? By this we mean, upon whom his subject has so acted,
that it has seemed to direct *him* – not to be arranged by him? Any upon
whom its leading or collateral points have impressed themselves so tyr-
annically, that he dared not treat it otherwise, lest he should falsify a
revelation? Any that has imparted to his compositions, not merely so
much truth as is enough to convey a story with clearness, but that individualising property, which should keep the subject so treated distinct
in feature from every other subject, however similar, and to common
apprehensions almost identical; so as that we might say, this and this
part could have found an appropriate place in no other picture in the
world but this?

CHARLES LAMB

As in the more modern pieces, we notice here the antithetical style. A distinction is drawn between the subject which directs the painter and the subject which is arranged by him; between 'clearness' and 'individualising'. These may be valid contrasts, but it would take more than this mode of classification to bring them out. The weight of emphasis lies on the terminology, not on the work ostensibly under discussion. The Belletrist tends to go in for poetic prose in lieu of citation.

The mode of the Prophet, while more intellectually respectable, may at times seem equally nebulous. Certainly it tends to invoke a good many abstractions. They may not, however, always be as abstract as they seem at first reading. Opinions about the extent of abstraction in any given example will be found to differ according to the extent to which the reader recognizes, behind the prose, the pressure of felt experience.

From: *English Literature in Our Time* (1969)

Life is growth and change in response to changing conditions, and modern civilization advances in the spirit of its triumphant logic at such a rate that the fact of change is taken for granted. It is taken for granted in such a way that the profounder human consequences and significances of unceasing rapid and accelerating change escape notice. The deduction I draw is that our time faces us with a new necessity of conscious provision: we have to make provision for keeping alive, potent and developing that full human consciousness of ends and values and human nature that comes to us (or should) out of the long creative continuity of our culture.

F. R. Leavis

'Life', 'growth', 'change', 'civilization', 'logic' and, again, 'change': you may well be forgiven if you take these words to be mere counters in lieu of a properly exploratory analysis of the nature of modern life or the facts of change. This critic has behind him a long record of writing and teaching – his first work many years previously. Moreover, behind this prose is a range of reference to previous authors – D. H. Lawrence, George Sturt, L. H. Myers – who felt that the process of living was being eroded by negative factors in modern society. However, younger readers, coming across the passage in question for the first time, may not know this: what is presented as self-evident conclusion they will see as argument, and therefore they will find the prose wanting in matter.

The tradition behind this kind of writing is strongly Victorian: the secular prophet has taken over from the Bible. He has the urgency, but also the isolation, of the voice in the wilderness.

From: *The Stones of Venice,* II vi (1851–52)

The great cry that rises from all our manufacturing cities, louder than their furnace blast, is all in very deed for this – that we manufacture everything there except men; we blanch cotton, and strengthen steel, and refine sugar, and shape pottery; but to brighten, to strengthen, to refine or to form a single living spirit, never enters into our estimate of advantages. And all the evil to which that cry is urging our myriads can be met only in one way: not by teaching or preaching, for to teach them is but to show them their misery, and to preach to them, if we do nothing more than preach, is to mock at it. It can be met only by a right understanding on the part of all classes, of what kinds of labour are good for men, raising them, and making them happy.

JOHN RUSKIN

Like Leavis, Ruskin is speaking out against the inroads upon living made by the character and growth of the manufacturing industries. We must beg the question as to whether the criticism is valid: certainly it has been firmly held by a number of critics. Our concern here is with the writer's efficacy in expressing his point of view. Ruskin is definitely more concrete than Leavis. Behind Leavis's reiterated 'changing conditions' and 'fact of change' are Ruskin's particulars of manufacture – we 'blanch cotton', we 'strengthen steel'. But even here there is a lack of close acquaintance which alone could guarantee the assertiveness of tone. It seems to me that this lack of acquaintance inevitably leads to the unbacked and pious hope for 'a right understanding on the part of all classes, of what kinds of labour are good for men'. This is what Monroe Beardsley calls Instrumentalism. We can all agree that we would like men to understand what kinds of labour are good for them; but how we are to agree upon the precise nature of that 'good', Ruskin does not tell us.

The Prophet tends to speak with sincere emotion ill-provisioned by specific fact. There are exceptions to this stricture, even in Ruskin; William Morris and Thomas Carlyle, too, can rise to great heights in the mode. But it is all too capable of being debased: the war speeches of Winston Churchill taught a generation of politicians how to be glibly oratorical, and a great many prophecies of our own time are couched in a prose such as this –

if there is one theme running through this conference, it is the theme of change, the overdue need for this country to adapt itself to different conditions...

or this –

We have had to face, and are still facing – and the way is going to be hard – the problems of economic change as some of our industries decline and we move over to the new ones...

This invokes the cry of change without even the pressure of implication which some of us can detect in Leavis. The speakers are Harold Wilson and Edward Heath, and they are performing at conferences of their parties in, respectively, 1963 and 1965. Their use of language, here as elsewhere, shows that it is not necessary to express oneself efficiently if one is to be a Prime Minister. Nothing could demonstrate more clearly the liability of having an imperfectly literate voting public and the need for as many of us as have the opportunity to attain as high a degree of literacy as possible.

No one did more to educate a literate minority than F. R. Leavis, but his work in that direction is not best exemplified by

his later, more prophetic, work. Rather he is at his best in handling language more elliptically. Paradoxically, it is in this way
that he achieves his individual kind of vividness. Here he is writing about *Othello*; but he does not do so directly. He chooses the
Victorian critic, A. C. Bradley, as a sort of butt representing a
viewpoint cited only to be discounted. This is highly characteristic of Leavis, and of the Critic as Ironist at large. The prose takes
on the character of dialogue: one voice vainly pontificating; the
other, in countering that pontification, evincing his own, super-
ior, point of view. Bradley says 'We must not call the play a tragedy of intrigue as distinguished from a tragedy of character'.
Leavis replies:

And we must not suppose that Bradley sees what is in front of him.
The character he is thinking of isn't Othello's. 'Iago's plot', he goes on,

> Iago's plot is Iago's character in action.

In fact the play (we need hardly stop short of saying) is Iago's character in action. Bradley adds, it is true, that Iago's plot 'is built on his
knowledge of Othello's character, and could not otherwise have succeeded'. But Iago's knowledge of Othello's character amounts pretty
much to Bradley's knowledge of it (except, of course, that Iago cannot
realize Othello's nobility quite to the full): Othello is purely noble,
strong, generous, and trusting, and as tragic hero is, however formid-
able and destructive in his agonies, merely a victim – the victim of
Iago's devilish 'intellectual superiority' (which is 'so great that we
watch its advance fascinated and appalled'). It is all in order, then, that
Iago should get one of the two lectures that Bradley gives to the play,
Othello sharing the other with Desdemona. And it is all in the tradition; from Coleridge down, Iago – his motivation or his motiveless-
ness – has commonly been, in commentaries on the play, the main
focus of attention.

This is vintage Leavis: 'Diabolic Intellect and the Noble Hero'
(1938), reprinted in a collection of essays, *The Common Pursuit*
(1952). It is a complex form of utterance and I should not advise
the aspirant critic to try it. But it has the virtues of strategy. In

showing how Bradley puts an undue weight on the intellect of Iago, Leavis gets across the idea that the tragedy lies in quite another direction, in Othello's lack of awareness about what is going on around him. He puts in perspective that quality most people recognize in Othello. He shows us the limitations of 'nobility'.

In Leavis's hands the ironic mode has many possibilities. It is in recent times that his fellow-critics have recognized his mastery of nuance. In our next example he applies his prose to a different problem and a different author. How alert and civilized was George Eliot? Leavis seizes upon a bêtise of Lord David Cecil's which seems to deny that great novelist qualities of alertness and civilization. By parodying Lord David Cecil's contentions, and by treating his book as an inexhaustible source of folly, Leavis contrives to put forward a persuasive case in George Eliot's favour. Lord David Cecil has said 'Like most writers, George Eliot could only create from the world of her personal exper- ience – in her case middle- and lower-class rural England of the nineteenth-century Midlands.' Leavis pretends to agree.

Moreover, she was confined by a Puritanism such as James (apart from the fact that he wasn't lower-middle-class) had left a generation or two behind him: 'the enlightened person of to-day must forget his dislike of Puritanism when he reads George Eliot'. Weighty, provinci- al, and pledged to the 'school-teacher's virtues', she was not qualified by nature or breeding to appreciate high civilization, even if she had been privileged to make its acquaintance. These seem to be accepted commonplaces – which shows how little even those who write about her have read her work.

This is from what may well be Leavis's most important book, his revaluing of the English novel, *The Great Tradition* (1947). Even from this passage we can see that the resentment felt against Leavis by the other critics was not, as was said at the time, because he was grudging in his literary advocacies. So far as creative wri- ters are concerned, he is generous and positive to a degree. He is, however, hard on the critics. The resentment against him was

provoked by his practice of using contemporary critics as characters in an unending comedy. Leavis has in this instance put
into the mouth of Lord David Cecil sentiments about George
Eliot which nobody would care to own. But one has to say that
Lord David Cecil lent himself to this: his unconscious class-pre-
judice and unfortunate tendency of phrase ('the school-teacher's
virtues') render him an all-too-vulnerable hostage to Leavis's
irony. But the end is not the dislodgement of Lord David Cecil,
who in any case has survived pretty well. Leavis used him, as he
has made use of other critics, to put forward the authors he ap-
preciates and wants us to appreciate. Behind the caustic display of
wit, there is a genuine humanity.

I suggested that *The Great Tradition* might be Leavis's most
important book, quite deliberately. It is hard for us now to realize how comparatively recent is serious criticism of the novel. Its
founding father was Henry James and he seems to have been
highly conscious of his role as pioneer. Indeed, he seems to have
been afraid of people thinking him too solemn. Therefore James
evolved an elaborate form of deference to his reader which has
the effect of checking the enthusiasm of the claims he makes for
the authors he recommends. Yet, oddly enough, this very check
upon enthusiasm makes for a highly persuasive descriptiveness
when it comes to drawing our attention to those authors' qualities.

From: 'Honoré de Balzac' (1902)

A born son of Touraine, it must be said, he pictures his province, on
every pretext and occasion, with filial passion and extraordinary
breadth. The prime aspect in his scene all the while, it must be added,
is the money aspect. The general money question so loads him up and
weighs him down that he moves through the human comedy, from beginning to end, very much in the fashion of a camel, the ship of the desert, surmounted with a cargo. 'Things' for him are francs and cen-
times more than any others, and I give up as inscrutable, unfathomable,
the nature, the peculiar avidity of his interest in them. It makes us won-

der again and again what then is the use on Balzac's scale of the divine
faculty.   `

HENRY JAMES

In refusing to claim for Balzac a higher spirituality, James
makes us aware of what the great novelist can do as a realist. At
first sight the urbanity of the style here may seem at an extreme
from the tart ingenuity of Leavis. But both critics work a
great deal through qualifications: Leavis, in the examples I gave
from his work, through parenthesis; James, in the example just
quoted, through progressive redefinition. You can see why I ad-
mire the mode and, at the same time, refuse to recommend it; at
least, not without a good many qualifications of my own. The
mode will work only in the hands of a mature master, and, on
the whole, most of us will have to content ourselves with being
straightforward.

In other words, ours is likely to be the prose of the Expositor.
Yet even this, as I indicated at the beginning, is not at all simple.
It is a matter for astonishment that universities require of their
students an ordered prose, as if to write in such a way were a
phenomenon frequent in nature. We can concede that the means
towards clear exposition lies in the hands of most literate people.
But the technique demands thought and this involves care, especially in revision, and such thought and care, in their turn, neces-
sitate a regard for the exigencies of one's medium. We will treat
that medium with respect if we remember that it has been the
chosen mode of some of the wisest and most learned men of our
time.

We have already looked at Impressionism in so far as it is manifest in the novel. Here is a reasoned attack on the Impressionist mode, in verse as well as prose, by one of the clearest-mind-
ed teachers of English in America.

From: Primitivism and Decadence (1937)

The so-called stream-of-consciousness convention of the contemporary novel is a form of qualitative progression. It may or may not be

used to reveal a plot, but at best the revelation can be fragmentary since the convention excludes certain important functions of prose – summary, whether narrative or expository, being the chief. It approximates the manner of the chain of thought as it might be imagined in the mind of the protagonist: that is, it tends away from the reconsidered, the revised, and tends toward the fallacy of imitative form, which I have remarked in the work of Joyce and of Whitman. It emphasizes, wittingly or not, abject imitation at the expense of art; it is technically naturalism; it emphasizes to the last degree the psychology of the hero, but the least interesting aspect of it, the accidental.

Yvor Winters

There are unfamiliar words here, as there were in the prose of the Belletrist, but they are definable. They are definable because – unlike the antithesis of consiliences and reverberations – they are necessary; they categorize concepts that were not separately recognized before the time of writing. To give such concepts names is therefore to extend our consciousness, and not in a Joycean way. 'Qualitative progression', narrative by emotional rather than by logical progression, is defined above, *in situ*. Winters goes on to define 'the fallacy of imitative form'.

This law of literary aesthetics has never that I know been stated explicitly. It might be thus formulated: Form is expressive invariably of the state of mind of the author; a state of formlessness is legitimate subject matter for literature, and in fact all subject matter, as such, is relatively formless; but the author must endeavor to give form, or meaning, to the formless – in so far as he endeavors that his own state of mind may imitate or approximate the condition of the matter, he is surrendering to the matter instead of mastering it. Form, in so far as it endeavors to imitate the formless, destroys itself.

Winters takes great pains to define something that clearly he very much dislikes. Nevertheless, the lucidity of his prose is such that, even if we have never considered the matter before, we become very well aware of it through his exposition. He is referring to aberrations like the attempt to write a chaotic poem as a means of portraying a chaotic universe, or boring the reader as a means of making him attend to a boring character.

It is difficult to speak of expository prose in terms that transcend its material content: it is essentially a faithful servant of the information to be conveyed. One could, however, point out, in Winters as in other authors, a recognizable decisiveness of sentence-structure. Each sentence, whatever its length, is governed by a single idea, and there is no indecision as to the subject. This is in the best tradition of our philosophic prose, and its greatest exemplar in the twentieth century is Bertrand Russell. He, too, seeks to define a concept where before there was vacancy. In the case I am about to quote, Russell is concerned with the peculiar fact that a sentence may seem to tell us something in faultless grammar and yet be demonstrably false.

From: 'On Denoting' (1905)

By a 'denoting phrase' I mean a phrase such as any one of the following: a man, some man, any man, every man, all men, the present King of England, the present King of France, the centre of mass of the Solar System at the first instant of the twentieth century, the revolution of the earth round the sun, the revolution of the sun round the earth. Thus a phrase is denoting solely in virtue of its *form*. We may distinguish three cases: (1) A phrase may be denoting, and yet not denote anything; e.g. 'the present King of France'. (2) A phrase may denote one definite object; e.g. 'the present King of England' denotes a certain man. (3) A phrase may denote ambiguously; e.g. 'a man' denotes not many men, but an ambiguous man. The interpretation of such phrases is a matter of considerable difficulty; indeed, it is very hard to frame any theory not susceptible of formal refutation. All the difficulties with which I am acquainted are met, so far as I can discover, by the theory which I am about to explain.

BERTRAND RUSSELL

There is an element of surprise in this prose. The list of possibilities that Russell gives as examples of denotation contain some oddities: the present King of France, and the revolution of the sun around the earth, among them. A good deal of apparently abstract philosophy is enlivened in this way by examples which may be poetic or even grotesque. Much of Russell's work in this area came out of his catechizing an obscure German philosopher, Meinong, who, in the course of denoting impossibilities, formulated the concept of the Golden Mountain. This is something which has a patent existence in the mind yet which cannot be said to 'exist' in 'the real world'. But the problem Russell is facing – the problem of the false sentence – is concrete enough, and this helps to give his prose its characteristic force and surge. For Russell, as for most thinking men, there is no gap between 'the real world' and the world of speculation; it is speculation that brings about the concept of the real world. In much the same way, the characters in a novel precipitate themselves through words into our minds and so become entities that we can talk about: Elizabeth Bennet, Clarissa Harlowe, Guppy, Krook, Betty Flanders, Stephen Dedalus. In this, criticism is a 'real' activity.

The difficulty for the aspirant is that some of the greatest critics have turned their activity into performance suited to their own peculiar sensibilities. Brilliant though James and Leavis are – and perhaps Lamb, too, in his highly individual way – we would be ill-advised to write like them. It is the old conundrum that one has to be a good deal like a person in order to take over his style. Therefore I should not advocate taking over even a style that I approve, be it that of Winters or that of Russell; not at least *ad hoc*. But I would say that these writers and their masters – Bacon, Locke, Mill – have virtues from which we can learn, and they are not virtues necessarily anchored to definitive personalities. They are rather qualities of expertise: lucidity, terseness, specificity. These seem to me qualities one would like to find in criticism and, indeed, in other forms of exposition. At any rate, we shall be liable to lose our audience without them.

V Writing notes

The breath of inspiration may guide the pens of the fortunate, but for most of us writing is hard work. It will seem even harder if the writing in question is not planned.

The basic subject of a critical essay is the text, and anything that is not about the text is open to scepticism. Biographical data, historical background, awareness of the author's philosophical position – all these may have their place in our studies. But they are relevant in criticism only to the extent that they illuminate the text.

It is inadvisable to use the text to illuminate the author unless you are writing a biography. Historical background must not usurp the foreground of the text, unless you are writing history. You should not, either, extrapolate from the author's work a system of thought; unless that author is a systematic thinker, and you intend to write philosophy.

If the text is at the heart of a discourse, a prime requisite for the person discoursing is possession of the text. By that I mean not only the purchase of a book but its frequentation. One prerequisite is knowing that you are going to study a book ahead of the time designated for its study. A first reading should take place well before the book in question comes up for discussion in lecture or tutorial.

One must avoid the sense of dispersion that seems to afflict many students on reading a book as text. All scenes are not equally important; some are climactic to the book as a whole; and that whole has an individual structure. The recognition of that structure is one of the techniques to which we must turn our attention.

In reading a text there is no intermediary except the incidental intervention of teacher or critic. To a considerable extent, what one wrests out of a book is a matter between oneself and the author. It is possible, under adverse circumstances, to read a book and to be left with nothing that could be termed an interpretation. This is not a fault of memory but a failure in the technique of reading.

Reading is a technique that develops with practice. One way of building up this technique is to make notes on what is read. This does not mean that you should make an elaborate summary of any set text, or break off in your reading in order to record a quantity of impressions. Rather than either of these practices, it would be better to make no notes at all until you have completed your reading of the whole. But, if you think yourself to be an inexperienced reader, it can do no harm to make just one or two notes after each chapter.

Suppose we take a text we have already glanced at in this book as an example; say, *Pride and Prejudice*. I had occasion to refer to an individual scene in Chapter 3; how would we set about writing notes upon the whole novel?

Let us assume that you have read the book through once. Begin your notes by writing a very brief summary of the plot. If the summary is more than six or seven lines long, it is a bad one. Something of this sort will do, and the technique may be adapted to any novel you read:

The hero is a young man of large fortune and fashionable manners, whose distinguishing characteristic is personal pride. The heroine, on the first introduction, conceives a most violent prejudice against Darcy, which a variety of circumstances well imagined and happily presented, tend to strengthen and confirm. Explanations of the different perplexities and seeming contrarieties, are gradually unfolded, and the two principal performers are happily united.

I had better confirm that this is not my own summary but that of one of the book's first admirers, a contributor to *The British Critic,* who reviewed *Pride and Prejudice* in 1813. The summary has the great merit of leaving out needless details in giving us an overall sense of the plot. A summary such as this might well be the first note you write about a novel once you have read it.

The error in remembering a book is to think of it as a host of competing scenes. In a literary masterpiece every scene has its place, but not all scenes are equally emphasized. Try to think in terms of five or six key scenes; those scenes that represent climaxes or hinges of the plot. No two readers will necessarily agree as to which scenes are climactic. But this does not matter provided you have attempted to make your own personal choice. The scenes you have chosen will be in the foreground of the book as you see it, and will help to determine its shape for you.

For example, in *Pride and Prejudice,* I personally would pick out the following scenes.

Volume I, Chapter iii	Longbourn. The Ball Scene, already looked at.
	Darcy: 'She is tolerable; but not handsome enough to tempt *me...*'
I xvi	Meryton. Wickham's narrative of his misfortunes at the hands of Darcy.
	Wickham: 'I should at this time have been in possession of a most valuable living, had it pleased the gentleman we were speaking of just now'. This prejudices Elizabeth further against Darcy. Darcy's pride is set off against Wickham's plausibility.
I xix	Longbourn. Collins's proposal to Elizabeth,

Collins: 'And now nothing remains for me but to assure you in the most animated language of the violence of my affection'. Contrast between sentiment and expression sets the fatuous Collins off against both Darcy and Wickham. Offer refused.

II xi

Collins marries Elizabeth's friend Charlotte and Elizabeth stays with them at Hunsford Parsonage. Darcy's proposal – 'I have no wish of denying that I did everything in my power to separate my friend [Bingley] from your sister [Jane] . . . Towards him I have been kinder than towards myself' – and rejection.

III iv

Darcy on his estate, Pemberley; hears Elizabeth's account of her youngest sister Lydia's elopement with Wickham; unexpected kindness. 'Elizabeth felt how improbable it was that they should ever see each other again on such terms of cordiality as had marked their several meetings in Derbyshire . . .'

III xvi

Longbourn. Darcy has helped Lydia, i.e. got her married to Wickham, and Elizabeth now accepts his proposal.

Darcy, referring to their early acquaintance:

'The recollection of what I then said, of my conduct, my manners, my expressions, during the whole of it, is now, and has been many months, inexpressibly painful to me.'

These scenes were all chosen with a high regard to considerations of plot. Another reader, one putting the emphasis more on character, might very well prefer other scenes. The Ball Scene would probably be common to both, and I think, too, that the scene of Mr Collins's proposal is crucial. But, with prime consideration for character, other scenes might be:

Volume I, Chapter i	Longbourn. Introduction to the Bennet family.
	Mrs Bennet: 'A single man of large fortune...What a fine thing for our girls!'
	Mr Bennet: 'How so? how can it affect them?'
II vi	Elizabeth's visit to Lady Catherine de Bourgh's seat, Rosings. 'When the ladies returned to the drawing-room, there was little to be done but to hear Lady Catherine talk...delivering her opinion on every subject in so decisive a manner as proved that she was not used to have her judgment controverted...'
II xviii	Longbourn. Lydia and the militia. 'She received an invitation from Mrs Forster, the wife of the colonel of the regiment, to accompany her to Brighton...She saw herself seated beneath a tent, tenderly flirting with at least six officers at once'.
III vi and vii	Longbourn. The return of Mr Bennet from his search for Lydia and Wickham, empty-handed.
	Elizabeth: 'You must not be too severe upon yourself'.
	Mr Bennet: 'I am not afraid of being overpowered by the impression. It will pass away soon enough'.

One way of starting a second reading of the book is to go to whatever scenes you have selected as climactic, these or others, and re-read them with close attention, noting the patterns of language especially. For example, in the Ball Scene, Darcy's own friend puts him in a light that invites prejudice. 'I hate to see you standing about by yourself in this stupid manner', says Bingley, though we ought to bear in mind that, in 1813, 'stupid' meant a temporary lapse in spirits rather than a permanent state of inanity. The language of Darcy in answer, however, approaches violence – 'You know how I detest it...it would be insupportable...you are wasting your time with me...' Through such language an initially unpleasing character is created.

If we take another example: in Mr Collins's proposal scene, the author does almost the impossible in rendering a dull and conceited man as a fascinating character. The joke lies in the fact that Collins is ludicrously unaware of the effect he has on other people. There is a gap between Collins's estimate of himself and that which is likely to be held by any reasonable person. The reasonable person is represented by Elizabeth. It is through her eyes that we mark the 'solemn composure' with which Mr Collins informs her that he is 'run away with by [his] feelings'. But the hiatus between the character's intentions and his effect upon the reasonable person is signalled to us by the words he uses.

I am not, of course, suggesting that these scenes should be looked at in isolation. After re-reading each scene intensively in the way I have indicated, it would be as well to consider it in context. We should think how each scene advances the plot, develops the characters, sets up an atmosphere, hinges upon the structure of the text as a whole. But the reader will imperfectly grasp the text as a whole if he is unaware of the qualities of specific scenes and the ways in which those scenes inter-relate.

Something of this approach can be adapted as an aid to the study of poetry. If you are confronted with a writer's Collected Poems, or even a selection of his work, the strategy is to make out of that *oeuvre* your own anthology. In the nature of things, all the poems will not appeal to you equally. Read through the volume and put a marker against those poems that interest you, that you want to re-read, or that puzzle you. Puzzlement may well be a manifestation of that quality I have elsewhere called resistance (*Theory of Communication,* 1970). There may be more happening in a poem than the conscious mind can take in at a first reading and the result may be an initial antipathy. But one seldom feels antipathy unless one's feelings have been worked upon, and this may well be a guarantee that further frequentation will uncover qualities unforeseen at first. The real barrier to further reading is not antipathy but indifference.

Once you have selected your personal anthology, try to establish which poems matter most to you; as with all texts, seek to possess them. This is best done by reading them aloud, trying to work out an interpretation. In some cases recording your performance on to a cassette machine and playing it back can be very useful. However, if circumstances do not admit of your reading aloud, try to hear the poem in question with the inner ear; read silently at the pace you would adopt under other conditions. Many of the people who complain that they do not like or do not understand poetry are reading it too quickly – at the pace they would read their morning newspaper. Therefore they miss the rhythm and so cannot hear the varying emphases the poet puts on different words. Too fast a reading will lose, also, crucial nuances of tone. Much of this can be avoided by committing poems to memory. The point was repeatedly made by the Victorian poet and critic, Matthew Arnold, who was also a school inspector. Further, it is much easier to learn off by heart what you like than what you don't like. Probably the best way of memorizing a poem is to rehearse several attempts towards an intelligent reading. A poem once memorized is possessed in a special way: it can be summoned to conscious attention at any time.

What happens with regard to longer poems? We had a look at an extract from 'The Epistle to Dr Arbuthnot' in Chapter 2. I am unrepentant at having dealt with this separately: it was conceived as an independent poem and preserves many signs of its separate structure. However, we have to learn very quickly that there are several ways of looking at any one work. The portrait of Atticus will not lose by being seen in a context.

In his later years Pope consciously imitated Horace. That is to say, he chose to recognize certain likenesses between his world of the 1730s and Horace's world in and around the court of Augustus Caesar, about 10 or 15 BC. His Imitations of Horace are free translations of the elder poet's work, and he prefaced them with a dedicatory letter to a friend, Dr Arbuthnot. This latter, though it makes various references to Horace, is an 'original' poem.

The Epistle as a whole falls into three parts. The first describes the way in which Pope, a poet of acknowledged eminence, is beset with inferior writers all clamouring for his help in order to further their careers. The second section describes the difficulties of his own literary life, and instances his clashes with various critics, patrons and libellers. These antagonists are typified by the characters Atticus, Bufo, and Sporus. The third section is a personal apologia: it states that he has shown restraint when put upon and therefore must not be blamed for his satire now.

Thus put baldly, the poem may seem to be literary in an inbred way. But this is not so. 'The Epistle to Dr Arbuthnot' is infused with a great range of emotion and this is expressed in a considerable variety of linguistic register.

The first section, lines 1–124, begins with a great onrush of words, mostly in a high (but not shrill) denunciatory tone.

> Shut, shut the door, good John! fatigu'd I said,
> Tye up the knocker, say I'm sick, I'm dead,
> The Dog-star rages! nay 'tis past a doubt.
> All Bedlam, or Parnassus, is let out:
> Fire in each eye, and Papers in each hand,
> They rave, recite, and madden round the land...

Once you have briefly summarized this section, in the manner indicated above, it might be as well to write notes on at least some of the key allusions. 'Dog-star', 'Bedlam', 'Parnassus' in lines 3 and 4 are representative instances. The allusions are part of Pope's meaning.

The Dog-star is Sirius, whose appearance was thought to cause great warmth upon earth and therefore to heat men's brains. It appeared most strikingly in late summer, a season which has traditionally been thought of as the Silly Season, when frivolous stories abound. It was also, in Ancient Rome, a season when people went in for poetry recitals. Therefore for Pope the Dog-star is a way of linking up Parnassus, which was sacred to the Muses who presided over the arts, and Bedlam, which was an asylum for the insane. In other words, Pope is saying that all poets are mad or that only madmen want to write poetry.

All this may seem quite learned. But the information, if one does not have it already, may be readily found in a Classical Dictionary or a moderate-sized encyclopaedia or an annotated edition of the work of the poet under discussion. The serious student would presumably have all of these. They will certainly help him in writing notes; and the writing of notes amounts to a small-scale critical introduction.

However, to write notes on every allusion, especially in a highly referential poem such as this one, would be a waste of time. One must avoid confusing one's interpretation with excessive detail. Nevertheless, some personal annotation is necessary, and deciding what one's notes should be is a useful exercise in criticism. That rare quality, commonsense, has to be the guiding principle. The poem begins 'Shut, shut the door, good John...!' So long as we recognize that 'John' is a servant rather than, say, Dr Arbuthnot himself, it does not matter whether or not we remember his surname is Serle. You will find it much more useful to recognize that the advice Pope gives the poetasters who beset him, 'Keep your piece nine years', derives from Horace's *Art of Poetry*. Horace goes on to say 'You can always destroy what you have not published, but once you have let your words go they cannot be taken back'.

This is one of the ways in which Pope represents himself as the Horace of his time. The representation would not work if Pope did not have the art and technique with which to sustain a role which in a lesser poet would be vainglorious. In support of this contention one could adduce the virtuosity with which the besieging poetasters are created – 'They rave, recite and madden round the land' – like an army of the insane. One could point to the easy sarcasm which presents Pope's foes in ridiculous postures –

> Nine years! cries he, who high in Drury-Lane
> Lull'd by soft Zephyrs thro' the broken Pane,
> Rymes e're he wakes, and prints before Term ends,
> Oblig'd by hunger and Request of friends...

The comedy lies in the hiatus between the poor circumstances of the poet and the mock-courtesy with which these are presented to us. It is akin to the humour which reduces coarse and lying flattery to a caricature of itself – 'I cough like Horace, and tho' lean, am short'. Horace had attributes other than these, but they are not such as the poetasters would understand. It is a way of saying that the poet who wrote these lines is, by virtue of his art, the Horace of his own, diminished, age.

One's understanding of the second section (lines 125–367) would be enhanced by writing notes on the three characters it puts forward. I have said that the portrait of Atticus would live if no such person as its prototype, Addison, were known to us. Yet it cannot do us any harm to know that Joseph Addison was the most distinguished man of letters between Dryden and Pope; that he held office in government under both Queen Anne and George I; that his play *Cato* was celebrated in its time as an example of classical tragedy and that he is now mainly known to us as the essayist who was co-author of the periodicals *The Tatler* (1709) and *The Spectator* (1711–12, 1714). Knowledge can never be a disadvantage if one has learned how to apply it. Only if one uses Pope's portrait as a means of assessing Addison will a knowledge of his life and work lead to irrelevance. But it will be as well to recognize that Pope takes up certain Addisonian traits, such as the great man's habitual presence at Button's Coffee-House, frequented also by lesser writers such as Thomas Tickell and Ambrose Philips.

Similarly, Bufo, according to the Twickenham edition of Pope, was a composite figure drawing upon characteristics of Bubb Dodington and the Earl of Halifax. Both of these were minor poets, eminent only for their social station. If Atticus represents the great writer who is flattered by his less able acolytes, Bufo represents the wealthy amateur flattered by his needy contemporaries. Both these figures stand in contradistinction to Pope, who represents himself as eminent through his talents, unapt to be flattered even though poor.

In spite of this Pope finds himself pilloried by the third figure portrayed in this section: Sporus. This, in its turn, was a lurid caricature of the bisexual Lord Hervey. Such knowledge can help us with lines like

> Now high, now low, now Master up, now Miss,
> And he himself one vile Antithesis.
> Amphibious Thing! that acting either Part,
> The trifling Head, or the corrupted Heart...!

The third section (368–419) is the shortest. At first sight, it seems the section most fraught with contemporary allusion. Yet a good deal of the point is that the allusions are no longer current. Pope tells us that he, the dreaded satirist, has in his time tolerated such writers as Dennis, Tibbald, Cibber, and Moore. Our reaction may well be to ask who these people are. But that is the point: their laurels have faded. Nobody reads them now.

> This dreaded Sat'rist Dennis will confess
> Foe to his Pride, but Friend to his Distress:
> So humble, he has knock'd at Tibbald's door,
> Has drunk with Cibber, nay has rym'd for Moor...

There would be no point in writing copious notes on these. A brief indication of their obscurity should be enough: a men-tion of one work by each, or one circumstance of each life, would do.

It is much more important to remember the Twickenham Edition's notes on the last lines, 406–19. Apparently Pope wrote these lines separately and sent them in a letter to a friend. It was his way of disclosing his mother's last illness. The lines therefore really amount to a brief elegy.

> O Friend! may each Domestick Bliss be thine!
> Be no unpleasing Melancholy mine:
> Me, let the tender Office long engage
> To rock the Cradle of reposing Age,
> With lenient Arts extend a Mother's breath,
> Make Languor smile, and smooth the Bed of Death...

They come appropriately as a close to an epistle whose third section shows Pope's resentment at scurrilous attacks upon his family. Earlier in the section he has written

> Let the two Curls of Town and Court abuse
> His Father, Mother, Body, Soul, and Muse.
> Yet why? that Father held it for a rule
> It was a Sin to call our Neighbour Fool,
> That harmless Mother thought no Wife a Whore, –
> Hear this! and spare his Family, James More!
> Unspotted Names! and memorable long,
> If there be Force in Virtue, or in Song...

The directness of utterance here and in the rest of this third section creates a sense of honest indignation. The Two Curls, diminished by being intertwined, together with the obscure James More, are reduced in the poem into spiteful traducers of a good man's family.

Taken as a whole, then, 'The Epistle to Dr Arbuthnot' is really a defence of Pope's literary life. I have taken note of two aspects: the shape of the poem as a whole, and the incidental allusions scattered throughout. But I have tried to relate these aspects to the language and indeed to the poetry of the work.

The apologia can only come across if we are conscious of the author's virtuosity.

This is also true of *Pride and Prejudice*. I would direct any student to write notes on the crucial scenes in the belief that deciding which these are is itself a worthwhile critical exercise. But of course several opinions on the matter are possible and this recognition in its turn can give rise to useful discussion. Such discussion will identify what is crucial to the book as a whole: insight into character, creation of personality through the deployment of language – the dismissive arrogance of Darcy, the self-aggrandizing diction of Collins.

So, though your notes should have a factual basis, the facts should be such as to help you towards a critical understanding of the text. We need not point out a character trait or an allusion only for the sake of trait or allusion. Such matters exist as essential details contributing to the effect of the work as a whole.

VI Structuring an essay

We are perpetually being asked to write essays about authors, but what is an author? So far as the literary student is concerned, an author is a body of work. Sometimes he can be a very large body indeed. How, in such a case, do we select what we are to talk about? How do we choose the points we have to make?

In the Papermac edition of Thomas Hardy's poems, edited by James Gibson, there are 949 titles. It is clear that, even if you read all these poems, you cannot write about them all.

However, in Chapter 5 I said that, in any given novel, some scenes were more crucial than others. This does not mean that any scene is dispensable. But on certain scenes the plot hinges, and quite often such scenes have a greater degree of emphasis than their fellows. They are, in short, foregrounded.

Therefore one tends to give them most attention, and this approach can be adapted with respect to a body of poems. Let us grant that there is no poem by Hardy with which we would care to dispense. There are still items in the total *oeuvre* which are classics, and we read the whole corpus of work to find out which these are. Such poems we read again and again, with close attention, marking every nuance of rhythm and meaning.

We make, in effect, a personal anthology. No two anthologies, it is true, will be exactly alike. A good deal depends on what circumstances condition the reading. There is a difference between reading at large and a reading angled to satisfy the requirements of a tutor. You may, in the latter instance, be asked to answer a specific question. Such a question may well determine the shape of your personal anthology. You may be asked to discuss Hardy's use of nature in his work. In such a case the spare landscaping of 'Neutral Tones' or 'The Darkling Thrush' could be put beside such great set-pieces as the description of Egdon Heath at the beginning of Hardy's novel, *The Return of the Native*. The shape of an essay on Hardy and Nature will, however, be quite different from one written upon another theme: Hardy and the Supernatural, say, or Hardy and Old Age. The range of options is reduced by the necessity of taking a line on Hardy's work. What you lose in width of application, you hope to gain in focus.

You may be given a negative sort of question on which to base your essay. The trend of criticism in the twentieth century has favoured impressionistic or metaphysical poets such as T.S. Eliot or Wallace Stevens, and it has shown distinct strain in seeking to assimilate Thomas Hardy. This strain is quite often seen in examination papers, almost as though the candidate is being asked to counter an adverse view of Hardy. You may find yourself being asked to defend (a) Hardy's metrical clumsiness or (b) his eccentric diction or (c) his tendency towards the prosaic or (d) his predilection for the obsolete and archaic. In such circumstances, clearly the examination candidate has a choice. You can, if you wish, attack Hardy, as you can any author put forward for detailed discussion. But such a negative approach tends to restrict the essay unduly. There is a distinct oddity in writing at length on a text only in order to get the reader to set it aside. Moreover, one always writes better about texts that one likes. It might therefore prove rewarding to turn the question against itself.

Let us look at objection (a) above. If one takes such metrical structures as 'Thoughts of Phena' or 'A Commonplace Day', it can be quite an engaging exercise to show how the elaboration and repetition in fact are expressive. Indeed, on frequentation, what seems a not always welcome originality comes to appear inevitable. With regard to objection (b), turns of phrase that look

odd out of context – 'stillicide', 'existlessness' – fall into place
when considered in the body of such poems as 'Friends Beyond'
or 'The Voice'. Once more, it is largely a question of rhythm; of
reading the poems aloud, of seeking to hear them. To counter
objection (c) it should be easy enough to justify the directness of
'I look into my glass'; the measured explicatory quality of 'A
Broken Appointment'; or the circumstantial detail of 'Beyond
the Last Lamp'. Objection (d), that Hardy was too much wedded to obsolete themes, could be countered by showing the wealth
of anecdote, of historical as well as narrative interest, embodied
in such poems as 'A Church Romance: Mellstock, *circa* 1835';
'The Oxen'; 'Old Furniture'; 'The Choirmaster's Burial';
'Retty's Phases'. In each and every case one should counter the
objections raised with poems by Hardy that you believe to be
good and interesting. In that way you can make a positive case
even out of a negative proposition.

There does not seem to be an adequate essay on Hardy's dialogue poems. These are a neglected side of his output. Yet here,
with a technique honed on the writing of prose fiction, he brings
to bear a non-lyrical register of language upon lyrical themes
and brings off a number of unexpected effects triumphantly.
Here again, one should match the generalized concept of 'dialogue poems' with specific examples, and it is these examples that
will give form and content to essay. Poems that come to mind
in this connexion include 'The Ruined Maid', 'The Workbox',
'Voices from Things Growing in a Churchyard'. The last displays
extraordinary ingenuity in creating the illusion of a whole com-
munity of the dead discoursing about life. Hardy sees the plants
which grow on and about the graves in a cemetery as bearing up-
ward into the air the traits of the characters buried in the soil.
Fanny Hurd says that she died young but

> now I wave
> In daisy shapes above my grave...

Bachelor Bowring who danced his life away now, in death, is 'a
dancer in green as leaves on a wall'. Thomas Voss has burrowed

into a yew, and Eve Greensleeves, once kissed by men, is now kissed by glowworms and bees. The flowers, leaves and plants are vegetable equivalents of those from whose remains they grow. They dance by day and by night – as the refrain has it,

> All day cheerily,
> All night eerily.

This could lead you on to a further essay, about refrains in Hardy or about the use Hardy makes of the ballad tradition. He was a very great poet indeed, and lends himself to many different critical approaches.

There is one aspect of Hardy's art likely to be discussed as long as English poetry is read. That is his use of the concrete image. Words like 'concrete', 'vivid', 'particular' are really abstractions: they express a twentieth-century distaste for the generalized and the vague. However, they have become so current in modern criticism that they are used as positive evaluations, without sufficient backing evidence. Yet it is no use saying that a poem is concrete unless you show it is concrete and why in that particular case concreteness is a quality to be admired. If this is done with regard to three or four of Hardy's poems, you have at least the makings of an appreciative essay.

In a poem written about 1900, 'The Self-Unseeing', Hardy at once looks back to a distant past and also sees himself through his ageing eyes as a child living in a historic present.

> Here is the ancient floor,
> Footworn and hollowed and thin,
> Here was the former door
> Where the dead feet walked in.
>
> She sat here in her chair,
> Smiling into the fire;
> He who played stood there,
> Bowing it higher and higher.
>
> Childlike, I danced in a dream;
> Blessings emblazoned that day;

Everything glowed with a gleam;
Yet we were looking away!

This poem has certain traits in common with 'During Wind and Rain' which we looked at in Chapter 2. It simulates reality by gripping on to particular circumstance. The tendency, in this poem and in others by Hardy, has much in common with the high-mimetic narrative we discussed in Chapter 3. What we can initially be certain of is the ancient floor 'footworn and hollow and thin'. But the qualifiers also prefigure the image of a ghost, and this is reinforced by the eerie phrase 'Where the dead feet walked in' – a phrase which contains what seems to be a paradox. Can dead feet walk? They could, if we were to take the term 'dead' to refer to a previous time: the *dead* feet which *then* walked. With this recognition, the poem slides back to the past. At that time – then – the poet was a child, and his present self remembers a past scene with the mother smiling into a fire and the father playing the fiddle. It is the difference between 'Here is' and 'She sat here'; the present tense and the past. In this way Hardy relates times far apart; relates them through place; and this is a characteristic of his finest poetry.

In looking at the concrete aspects of Hardy, one could seek to indicate that he tends to use particularity as a way of rendering concrete retrospective and even supernatural aspects of his theme. He calls back the dead, as memory or ghost, as living embodiments in a context which counteracts any suggestion that they are alive. In 'Logs on the Hearth', what is being burned is the tree that the poet and his sister climbed when they were children. It is now 'sawn, sapless, darkening with soot'; about as dead as it could be. Yet in the firelight Hardy evokes the memory of that long-dead sister, and she seems alive –

My fellow-climber rises dim
   From her chilly grave –
Just as she was, her foot near mine on the bending limb,
   Laughing, her young brown hand awave.

The evocation of individual characteristics, such as 'her young brown hand awave', makes these dead seem to live. It is also a way of coalescing the past and present experience. This point, in its turn, will suggest another line of argument, and another essay. The limitation of essay structure is such that these lines cannot all be explored. Half the strategy is in deciding what line to take. In theory it would be possible to write a whole essay on a single poem or even, with a work of the stature of 'After a Journey' or 'At Castle Boterel', on a single aspect of a poem. However, you have to ration what you say. You may choose your various points in such a manner as to link them together under one head or another: thematic tendency, linguistic texture, sense of the past, basic construction – to name only a few of the possibilities. The nub of all that has been said is this: criticism is an art of selection.

This is no less so when the student is confronted with a single work written on a large scale. There are difficulties in interpreting *Paradise Lost, The Prelude, The Faerie Queene, Bleak House* or *Tom Jones*. Such works have so many words that it is not easy to remember how they are all related. But there are techniques for discussing such works as these.

One could try to begin with making out a very terse summary: the same approach as was adumbrated in the previous chapter. The story of *Tom Jones,* for instance, could be encapsulated in the following way:

Book 1, Chapter 2	Introduction. The widower Allworthy and his spinster sister, Bridget.
1.3	Allworthy finds a baby in his bed.
1.4, 1.5	Bridget is delighted with the baby; her maid, Deborah, is not.
1.6	Local girl Jenny Jones is supposed to be the mother and admits to the supposition.
1.7	Allworthy arranges for her to leave the village. She refuses to name the father.
1.8	Bridget Allworthy discourages her maid Deborah's curiosity about the baby.

1.9	Local opinion believes Allworthy to be the father and turns against Jenny.
1.10	Allworthy maintains as house guests first a Dr Blifil, then also his brother, a half-pay officer.
1.11	Bridget accepts Captain Blifil for her future husband.
1.12	They marry.
1.13	Captain Blifil drives out his brother

et cetera. But a treatment of the book as a whole on this scale would be excessively long-drawn-out. *Tom Jones* presents a structure markedly different from that of *Pride and Prejudice*. To summarize in this manner here will tend to obscure the narrative with detail. One might carry on with the summary as a species of raw material: a kind of memorandum for private consultation. But it cannot, as it stands, be the basis of an essay. What is called for, rather, is a version of the technique employed in Chapter 2 for looking at poems. One needs to look for a core, a centre, a dominating issue.

At first sight, this will not seem easy. As Dr Leavis said, some episodes of *Tom Jones* take place in the country and some in town, some in the churchyard and some in the inn, some on the high-road and some in the bed-chamber, and so on. Nevertheless, there is an order in the book, and it will become apparent through acquaintance with the text.

One approach is to take *Tom Jones* to be, at its core, a gigantic folk-tale. It has many of the marks: the unrecognized heir, the wandering hero, the quest for the heiress, the contest between hero and villain. All of these are recognizable components in fairy-literature, and this is to suggest that they form the basis of many more modern narratives. One of the most useful aids in this form of analysis is *Morphology of the Folktale* by Vladímir Propp, a highly sophisticated account of the structure of primitive stories. Using Propp's terminology you could break down the structure of *Tom Jones* in such a way as to get an idea of the function of various key incidents. The first column below is a codified means of classifying a phase in a story. The second column gives that classification a name. The third column defines the classification in such a way as to relate it to other tales. The fourth column relates it specifically to *Tom Jones*. The fifth column indicates the chapter or chapters in *Tom Jones* where the incident in question takes place.

Number	Designation	Propp's Definition	Summary of TOM JONES	Chapter
a	lack	One member of a family desires to have something	Tom Jones wants Sophia	4.13, 5.2
L	unfounded	False claim presented by the false hero	Blifil finds out Tom's parentage and conceals his knowledge; tells lies about Tom because he wants Sophia himself	5.8, 6.4, 6.10
↑	departure	The hero is dispatched from home as a result of the false claim	Tom Jones is sent away by Allworthy for his presumption in paying court to Sophia and ingratitude to his benefactor	6.11
D	the first function of the donor	A hostile creature attacks the hero	Tom is laid low by a blow from Ensign Northerton	7.12
F	provision of an agent	As a result of D, a character places himself at the hero's disposal	Partridge binds Tom's wound and offers to accompany him in his travels	8.6
G	guidance	Hero is led to the heiress	Tom finds himself in the same inn as Sophia at Upton	10.6
H	struggle	Hero and villain engage in competition	Squire Western, Sophia's father, attempts to have Tom arrested	10.7
I	victory	Villain defeated in competition	Magistrate acquits Tom	10.7
o	unrecognized arrival	Hero arrives in another country	Tom reaches London in search of Sophia	12.14
M	difficult task	Test of endurance	Tom makes love to Lady Bellaston and is supplied by her with money	13.7

D	the second function of the donor	Another hostile creature attacks hero	Fitzpatrick fights Tom, is wounded; Tom seized and imprisoned	16.10
J	branding	Hero receives a wound in skirmish	Tom branded as murderer	17.2
Q	recognition	Hero recognized after previous period of separation	Mrs Waters (Jenny Jones) tells Mr Allworthy Tom's true parentage; Tom really his nephew	18.7
Ex	exposure	What has occurred exposes the false hero in his true colours	As a result of Mrs Waters's story and the lawyer Dowling's confirming evidence, Allworthy realizes the badness of Blifil's nature	18.8
T	transfiguration	By means of the action of a helper, the hero effects a new appearance	As a result of Mrs Waters's intervention Tom, now discharged from prison, is reinstated with Mr Allworthy	18.10
U	punishment	The false hero is punished	Tom conveys Mr Allworthy's notice of expulsion to Blifil	18.11
W	wedding	The hero marries the heiress and comes into his heritage	Tom marries Sophia and takes over Western's hall	18.13

This is by no means the final shape of an essay; but it has the merit of indicating a way through the immense labyrinth of Fielding's plot. The diachronic structure of narrated events, that is to say the incident-by-incident sequence of plot, is only one dimension. Another is the synchronic structure; that is, the logic that relates the plot you are studying to other plots. There are many more incidents possible to a tale than are found in *Tom Jones*. Not all are found in any one tale. Those that are found determine the kind of tale it is. For example, it is quite important that the wandering figure of Tom Jones takes up with a friendly agent or helper, the barber-surgeon Partridge. It may not be accidental that this agent has the name of a non-human creature. In folk-tale after folk-tale the hero is accompanied in his travels by an affable beast. We think, for example, of Dick Whittington and his cat; and, like those two, Tom and Partridge reach London and make their fortunes. Another synchronic relationship is with that order of folktale in which an apparently low-born hero courts a princess. He is often found to be a prince himself and so the interdict that barred his marriage is lifted. As Mr Allworthy's nephew and heir, Tom has access to Sophia Western in a way impossible to one low-born and illegitimate.

A further structure of narrative, and hence of essay, may be defined through the function of the various characters. The status in the plot of the hero and of the heiress is clear enough in any plain survey, whether it is the précis sketched out first or the structural analysis projected after the method of Vladímir Propp. But the latter suggests some form of order among the more negative characters. Ensign Northerton and Mr Fitzpatrick are donors: they bring the hero luck even though their intentions towards him are hostile. The attack by Northerton is the cause of Tom's acquaintance with Partridge, first in his capacity as surgeon, then as travelling companion. The attack of Fitzpatrick directly leads to Tom's recognition as nephew, heir and worthy suitor. There is a difference between their antagonism and the role of Squire Western. The latter acts like a fairytale ogre or villain. He is instrumental in getting Tom expelled from Mr Allworthy's house in the first place and, later on, he tries to get him put in prison at Upton. Poetic justice dictates that he suffers in a way that Northerton and Fitzpatrick do not. At the end of the book he is deprived both of his daughter and his hall. In a real sense Tom deprives him of his place, though the punishment is only partial: he retains visiting rights. His conduct has not been as reprehensible as that of – to keep to Propp's terminology – the False Hero. Adapting that terminology to *Tom Jones,* it can be seen that Blifil attempts to supplant Tom as Allworthy's heir and Sophia's suitor. Therefore he is punished; not with partial banishment, like Western, but with a banishment that is total. Indeed, salt is rubbed into his wounds by the fact that it is Tom who bears the fatal message that his fortunes have changed irrevocably for the worse. However, since *Tom Jones* is a novel despite its affinity with the folk-tales, we are given a hint at the end that Blifil has some hope of repairing his fortunes in a sphere where his villainy will be appreciated.

Tom Jones is a novel: this suggests that Propp's mode of structural analysis is the beginning of criticism rather than the whole of the story. One has to relate to the text more sharply even than has been done in the discussion so far. There is a further mode of structural analysis: in this particular case, Dorothy Van Ghent points out that even the linear narrative, the diachronic sequence of narrated events, has a definite shape. 'There have been six books of country life, in the centre are six books of life on the highways, and the final six books are concerned with life in London.' This may give a clue as to how to achieve a really defined discussion of the book. 'From the central scenes at Upton Inn, the novel pivots around itself. . .it is at Upton Inn, in the mathematical mid-point of the story, that the country and city come together.'

You should be sure that you have grasped the linear spine of the story, whether by making a straightforward summary of the salient facts of the novel or a structural analysis after the manner of Propp. But you should also remember that your tutors and examiners have read the novel, too, and that they are likely to want you to talk about those aspects of it related to whatever questions they have asked you. Quite a number of possible questions about Fielding will be found to bear upon the form or otherwise of this picaresque novel, *Tom Jones*. In other words, a central query about the book will relate to whether the wanderings of the central figure – the picaro, the apparent plaything of fortune – can be construed in such a way as to suggest a definite narrative shape. We could therefore do worse than take up this hint from Dorothy Van Ghent and start, not at the beginning of the novel, but at the centre, the core. We can formulate an essay by joining Tom at Upton; between Chapters 9.3 and 10.7 of *Tom Jones*.

We find in this section that a surprising number of the characters of the book have converged. Some have been introduced before the Upton scenes, some come into their own afterwards. Tom and Sophia are under the same roof for the first time since 6.8. In that chapter she had told him that she would refuse Blifil but that she could not go so far against her father's intention as to bestow herself on Jones. Even now, they are only in the most literal sense under the same roof; for they do not meet. Indeed, they are the poles between which oscillate a series of fast-moving situations.

Tom has rescued Mrs Waters from Ensign Northerton who was trying to murder her. He does not know her to be the former Jenny Jones, his putative mother; nor does she know him. So there is nothing much to stop Tom from succumbing to her charms and landing in bed with her (9.5). This is the climax of the Upton episode; for this encounter suddenly becomes everybody's business.

A Mr Fitzpatrick, of great importance later on when he attacks Tom (16.10), arrives at the inn seeking his wife. The inn's maidservant has heard enough talk of Mrs Waters to imagine, erroneously, that she is the lady in question. This maidservant therefore leads the enraged Fitzpatrick straight into Mrs Waters's bedchamber. There the fiery Irishman finds the lady he takes to be his wife in bed with a gentleman, and immediately proceeds to blows. This arouses the house, but Mrs Waters manages to pass off the predicament by denouncing Tom, Fitzpatrick, and a friend of Fitzpatrick's who has also come in, as rapists and murderers. Tom connives at the ruse by making an apology to Mrs Waters for having appeared before her in his shirt, assuring her 'That nothing but a concern for her safety could have prevailed on him to do it'. By this means Mrs Waters is able to establish a new role, 'that of a modest lady, who was awakened out of her sleep by three strange men in her chamber'. Fielding, in other words, plays upon the irony generated by the gap between what the landlady and Mr Fitzpatrick are led to believe and what we know. There is a further irony beyond this,

since we do not know as much as we think. The identity of Mrs
Waters is still kept from us, not to be revealed until 18.2.

Another effect Fielding is adept at producing is a sort of peripeteia or turnaround. No sooner do we think that Tom is safe
and all well than a fresh circumstance renders all ill again. We
must remember that, unknown to Tom, Sophia and her maid
have arrived at this same inn, fleeing from Squire Western, *en
route* to a female relation in London. Sophia's maid gets talking
with Partridge, and discovers that not only is Tom upstairs but
that he is in bed with another lady. The fact is confirmed by the
talkative maidservant, she that showed Fitzpatrick into the bed-
chamber. Sophia resolves to go away forthwith but leaves her
muff behind with her name pinned on it to show Tom that she
knows what he has been up to. This muff has figured quite pro-
minently in the novel so far and is a kind of emblem for the
young lady herself. It is mortifying for Tom to find this, and he
is about to leave in pursuit, when Sophia's father, Squire Western, arrives in chase of his daughter and finds Tom *in flagrante
delicto,* with Sophia's highly identifiable muff in his hand. Fitzpatrick steps forward in the full knowledge that the woman Tom
was with in bed is not Mrs Fitzpatrick, and from this makes the
entirely wrong assumption that she must therefore have been the
squire's daughter. He ushers Western into the bedroom, disturbing Mrs Waters for the second time that night. Whoever else
Mrs Waters may be, she certainly is not Sophia, and so the
squire has to reduce his charge to accusing Tom of stealing the
muff. Here we have Western playing the part of ogre or villain:
the heavy father is in competition with the hero. But a further
peripeteia ensues. The inn's maidservant, coming down at last
on the hero's side of the matter, deposes that Sophia sent Tom
the muff voluntarily, and so Squire Western is defeated in this
particular contest. Everybody, apart from the people of the inn,
leaves in different directions. Western and Tom go their diverse
ways in pursuit of Sophia. Mrs Waters leaves in company with
Mr Fitzpatrick, and manages to fill the vacant place of his wife.

Through all this Fielding keeps up a judiciously distanced

style, and much of the effect is owing to the extent that it is at odds with the farcical violence of the action. This is a deliberate technique on Fielding's part. It is an effect that keeps the action at a fairly low level of mimesis, and so adds an edge at once to the humour and the irony. It is a form of mythopoeia: the rendering of action as legend or, as Fielding himself called it, comic epic in prose. It suggests that the author himself was very well aware of the archetypal or folk elements he had incorporated into his fiction. 'Thus ended the many odd adventures which Mr Jones encountered at his inn at Upton, where they talk, to this day, of the beauty and lovely behaviour of the charming Sophia, by the name of the Somersetshire angel.'

A good deal of the irony can be understood fully only on a second reading. There is an obvious irony in the difference between the semblance of Mrs Waters, upon the first intrusion into her room, and the reality; between a lady outraged by the trespass of three rough men and the jolly adventuress who has been enjoying the favours of one of them all evening. We may see the humour in finding ourselves wiser than the landlady and Mr Fitzpatrick. But there is a further irony, into which we are not admitted on first reading the book, that she is really Jenny Jones, thought to be the mother of Tom Jones, and therefore unknown to herself committing incest. This is what, in a characteristically ingenious essay, Sir William Empson called a double irony. However, there is a further irony yet in the fact that the imputation is false, and that, unknown to any first reader until the denouement of 18.7, Jenny Jones merely consented to a stratagem in order to conceal the identity of the true mother: Bridget Allworthy. So we have a kind of ironic layer-cake. Naughty Mrs Waters goes to bed with a young man; when interrupted she becomes virtuous Mrs Waters surprised by three young men; later on it seems that she was unwitting but guilty Jenny Jones in bed with her son; later on still, it seems that in fact she was naughty Jenny Jones in bed with a young man whom she does not know to be the foundling whom she acknowledged, in order to protect another.

Yet another approach is possible. A related strategy is to look at the novel as a process of demystification. Such a strategy might well start with this basic datum:

Mr Allworthy had been absent a full quarter of a year in London on some very particular business, though I know not what it was; but judge of its importance by its having detained him so long from home, whence he had not been absent a month at a time during the space of many years. He came to his house very late in the evening, and after a short supper with his sister, retired much fatigued to his chamber. Here, having spent some minutes on his knees – a custom which he never broke through on any account – he was preparing to step into bed, when, upon opening the clothes, to his great surprise he beheld an infant, wrapt up in some coarse linen, in a sweet and profound sleep, between the sheets...(1.3)

We start the book with a mystery: who is the child? Further, where are his parents? Further still, who put the child in Mr Allworthy's bed and why? The book may be taken as a progressive series of movements in the direction of unveiling these mysteries. Not all is mysterious: we know that Mr Allworthy is a widower whose children died in infancy and we have seen him to be deeply religious and basically kindly. Therefore it is reasonable to suppose that he will take care of the infant. It is not surprising to find him 'owning a resolution to take care of the child, and to breed him up as his own'. What is more surprising is to find that his sister, Miss Bridget Allworthy, takes the good-natured side of the question and commends her brother's charity, for we are told that she is a severe character with a great regard for what the ladies are pleased to call virtue. This is an odd circumstance; taken together with the fact that Mr Allworthy has been away for some time, it gives a clue to the origin of the foundling. This clue, however, is not sufficient to dispel the need for the stripping away layer after layer of mystery. In its turn, such a stripping away may provide you with a possible approach to the book and be the basis of an essay on the subject.

The clues manifest themselves on repeated frequentations of

the novel, and this is what makes it a classic. You cannot exhaust the possibilities of *Tom Jones* in a single reading. Indeed, re-reading such a work is as important as reading it. On re-reading, certain effects fall into place and become attitudes. Tom Jones, as Sir William Empson has remarked, possesses few friends, and those are mostly fairly low on the social scale, like Black George, the thieving gamekeeper. Therefore it is impressive that Tom grows up with what are basically good impulses. He makes mistakes but he is free of faults such as meanness and slyness. This is a suggestion that his heredity is sound. However, we do not know this for a fact until the final dénouement in 18.7. Tom's father is never a presence in the book until invoked retrospectively as the son of a friend of Mr Allworthy's, a Mr Summer, who died young. Because of this, there is never a chance of the clues laid by Fielding giving us any genuine help in demystifying the narrative. Only reading the book right through can do that. It is almost as though Fielding were afraid of our being able to anticipate his conclusion.

This point, in its turn, could lead you on to a moral consideration of the novel. The hero, in order to survive in London, makes love to the old and smelly Lady Bellaston (13.7, 13.8, *et seq.*). This renders him a kept man; and what are the rights and wrongs of that? In pondering this aspect of the novel, other considerations come into play. Some of them are minor: for example, Tom has promised to join the army (7.11) but in fact goes after Sophia as soon as he has a clue as to her whereabouts (10.6).

Let us develop this approach. He is represented as generous: he takes punishment on behalf of Black George the gamekeeper as well as himself (3.2); he gives away more than half the money which a highwayman whom he has captured was attempting to take from him (12.14); he forgives Blifil (18.11). He is also courageous: he tries to rescue Sophia's bird (4.3); he saves Sophia in a riding accident (4.13); he rescues the Man of the Hill from robbers (8.10), Mrs Waters from Ensign Northerton (9.2), a Merry Andrew from his master (12.8) and defends himself vigorously against Mr Fitzpatrick's onslaught (16.10). He is, further, chivalrous: he is genuinely in love with Sophia (5.2 *et seq.*) and he objects to Northerton insulting her (7.12); he intercedes with Nightingale on behalf of a girl whom he has seduced and intends to abandon (14.4, 14.7); he refuses to marry a rich widow for money (15.11); he refuses Mrs Fitzpatrick's advances (17.9), even though he knows she is estranged from her husband and he is sure he has no chance with Sophia.

But, on the other hand, Tom is wild. He gets irresponsibly drunk in order to celebrate Mr Allworthy's recovery from illness (5.9) and so plays right into Blifil's hands. He carelessly loses the money Mr Allworthy has given him on sending him away from home (5.12). He is also lecherous: making love to Molly Seagrim both before declaring himself to Sophia (4.6), and after (5.10); he makes love to Mrs Waters (9.5), and to Lady Bellaston (13.7). How, then, do we retain our general sense that Tom is a hero deserving our sympathy? Perhaps Tom's own remarks regarding the virtuous girl whom Nightingale has injured are pertinent here. '"I am no canting hypocrite, nor do I pretend to the gift of chastity more than my neighbours. I have been guilty with women, I own it, but am not conscious that I have ever injured any."' This key statement is backed up by Fielding's general process of narrative: Molly Seagrim, it turns out, was made pregnant by one Will Barnes before Tom ever saw her; Mrs Waters is a lady of easy virtue anyway; Lady Bellaston has an evil reputation. Moreover, all these experienced ladies made the first advances to Tom and, though he succumbs to them, it is he who in greater or lesser measure suffers. Therefore Fielding achieves the effect of Tom Jones being a good enough young man without having to whitewash him – as Richardson does Sir Charles Grandison – into unearthly purity.

With a didactic text, such as *Tom Jones* necessarily is, you do not need to go into intricate verbal detail. The sort of interest such detail would afford is often a small part of the effect. The prose of such a work is generally denotative, written for sense and perspicuity rather than (as with Dickens) for powerful local

suggestion. The difference is that between the distanced introduction to Allworthy that we looked at in Chapter 3 and the
dramatic presentation of the guilt and fear of the conspirators
in Dickens's *Bleak House,* discussed in the same chapter.

I hope that this has shown a number of ways into *Tom Jones*
and so a number of approaches towards structuring essays on
that text. I hope, also, what I have said about one particular text
may be taken as a set of working possibilities capable of being
adapted with regard to others. Whether one discusses a book in
terms of structure, demystification, irony or morality, the result
should be an essay designed to throw light upon the subject.
That there are difficulties in discussing large-scale works I know
from experience. However, if you bear in mind that the process
is one mainly of selection, all should go well. Not all scenes are
equally important, nor are all characters. The technique is to
consider climactic points after a first reading of the book. Probably even with that degree of selection you will find yourself with
too many points for a single essay. But the attempt to answer a
specific question, either in an examination or for a tutorial,
should bring some points into play more than others.

The construction of an essay, in other words, involves the
breaking down of a large-scale text into its discussible aspects,
and that involves a decision on your part about what you want
to discuss. I use the term 'breaking-down' because there can be
no final word on the matter. The essay is not there to replace the
text. By choosing a particular approach to a text you are giving
yourself a chance of seeing how it works in its component parts.
You are therefore giving yourself a chance to see how it is put
together.

VII Background and biography

So far, for the most part, we have been discussing texts on their own, with little regard for the raw material that went into them. This approach has the virtue of simplicity, but there is a degree of impressionism latent in such a discussion. One is advancing claims for a particular text, and one's conception of (say) its concreteness or irony can be backed up by adducing specimens of texture and putting them forward for analysis. Yet the analysis is partial: one cannot quite escape the imputation of talking in a void.

Over the years I have found it more and more useful to look at a text in juxtaposition with the source material: either the raw anecdotage from which literature surprisingly often is refined, or the literary work that most probably acted as influence. It cannot be too strongly emphasized that no writer emerges fully-blown: he has to go to school, to serve an apprenticeship, and that apprenticeship is usually dominated by a particular master.

For example, in Chapter 2 I adduced a poem, 'They flee from me', by Sir Thomas Wyatt. I put it forward as a great poem in its own right and also as an example of the best that the sixteenth century in England could do – a poem admirable of its period. I also hoped that my discussion would be an example of a way into a literary text; in particular, I sought to stress the importance of the centre, core or dominance in a poem. What I did not do was to suggest the poem's provenance: I did not, at that point in my general argument, lay any stress on where the poem came from.

In some ways it would be true to say that the poem came from the author's head. But that in itself suggests a cerebral quality in writing. A text of any kind is a highly artificial production; elements of tradition and technique form a large part of its composition; and these can, in my opinion, be usefully pointed out as part of our total appreciation. It is true that an effective text is largely self-sufficient: one can never replace a reader's experience with a whole lot of notes. If the text does not, to some extent, speak to us, no amount of explanation is going to work in its stead. At the same time, appreciation can be sharpened if we set the source beside the text.

'They flee from me' seems so original a poem that for a long time it was thought to be unique to Wyatt. Even within his output, it differs from the formal lute-songs and Petrarchan sonnets that form so large a proportion of his *oeuvre*. But in 1963 C. E. Nelson established that some of the unusual quality of the poem was due to the influence of Ovid.

Amores III vii remains untranslated in the Loeb edition, and this is a sign of the primness of an earlier generation. It is an impotency farce. The lover has got the girl to bed but he cannot perform. Ovid says

> *At non formosa est, at non bene culte puella,*
> *at puto non votis saepe petita meis!*
>
> *hanc tamen in nullos tenui male languidus usus*
> *sed iacui pigro crimen onusque toro*
>
> *nec potui cupiens, pariter cupiente puella,*
> *inguinis effeti parte iuvante frui.*
>
> *illa quidem nostro subiecit eburnea collo*
> *brachhia, Sithonia candidiora nive,*
>
> *osculaque inseruit cupide luctantia linguis*
> *lascivum femori supposuitque femur*
>
> *et mihi blanditias dixit dominumque vocavit*
> *et quae praeterea publica verba iuvant...*

Early in the 1580s, while he was still an undergraduate, Christopher Marlowe translated this as

> Either she was foul, or her attire was bad,
> Or she was not the wench I wish'd t'have had.
> Idly I lay with her, as if I lov'd not,
> And like a burden griev'd the bed that mov'd not.
> Though both of us perform'd our true intent,
> Yet could I not cast anchor where I meant.
> She on my neck her ivory arms did throw,
> Her arms far whiter than the Scythian snow,
> And eagerly she kiss'd me with her tongue,
> And under mine her wanton thighs she flung.
> Yea, and she sooth'd me up, and call'd me 'Sir',
> And us'd all speech that might provoke and stir...

This is a direct description of a failed amorous encounter. Wyatt turned it to dramatic effect by a technique of allegory. He loses no sense of the particular in making us feel that this downfall is part of a general reverse. He begins with this reverse –

> They flee from me, that sometime did me seek
> With naked foot, stalking in my chamber...

There is a flashback to the time when he was successful –

> Thanked be fortune it hath been otherwise
>   Twenty times better; but once, in special,
> In thin array, after a pleasant guise,
>   When her loose gown from her shoulders did fall,
>   And she me caught in her arms long and small...

In other words, Wyatt draws upon Ovid's description of sexual encounter in order to create a general, not a local, sense of impotence. Perhaps D. W. Harding, distinguished psychologist as well as critic, was right when he suggested that the form of the love lament offered indirect expression to a range of feeling that might have arisen from quite other sources, such as the reversal of Wyatt's position at court owing to the fluctuation of the

King's regard or the intrigues of his various rivals. Certainly the effect is one of general downfall, not of one particular failure with one particular girl. Fortune who gives will take away –

> *tacta tamen veluti gelida mea membra cicuta*
> *segnia propositum destituere meum.*
>
> *truncus iners iacui, species et inutile pondus,*
> *et non exactum corpus an umbra forem.*
>
> *quae mihi ventura est, siquidem ventura, senectus*
> *cum desit numeris ipsa iuventa suis?*
>
> *a pudet annorum, quo me iuvenemque virumque?*
> *nec iuvenem nec me sensit amica virum.*
>
> *sic flammas aditura pias aeterna sacerdos*
> *surgit et a caro fratre verenda soror...*
>
> (OVID)

> Yet like as if cold hemlock I had drunk,
> It mocked me, hung down the head, and sunk.
> Like a dull cipher or rude block I lay,
> Or shade or body was I, who can say?
> What will my age do, age I cannot shun,
> When in my prime my force is spent and done?
> I blush, that being youthful, hot and lusty,
> I prove neither youth nor man, but old and rusty.
> Pure rose she, like a nun to sacrifice,
> Or one that with her tender brother lies...
>
> (MARLOWE)

> It was no dream; I lay broad waking:
>> But all is turned, through my gentleness,
> Into a strange fashion of forsaking;
>> And I have leave to go of her goodness,
>> And she also to use newfangleness...
>
> (WYATT)

We have the material here for a two-way, if not a three-way, comparison. But the critical strategy would be to use the other

poems on this theme as foils to 'They flee from me'. Such a procedure could not but work greatly to Wyatt's advantage. The
Ovid love lament which the Loeb editor refused to translate, the
Marlowe translation which the public hangman burned in 1599,
suffer from their individualism and explicitness. It does not matter whether a youth is impotent with a particular girl: at least, it
is hard to make it matter to us. Wyatt, on the other hand, shows
something that touches us all: setback, disappointment, hopes
confounded, the fickleness of fortune. The eerie beginning may
have learned from Ovid – 'They flee from me, that sometime did
me seek'. But it far transcends Ovid in proverbial sharpness,
resonant overtones and a sense of relating the particular to the
general. In this way Wyatt matches his experience to our own, to
that of the world. There is nothing in Ovid or Marlowe to equal
the sense of place that we find in Wyatt: 'With naked foot, stalking in my chamber'. That 'stalking' gives the sense of beings
– girls, friends, mice in the prisoner's cell – once gentle, in all
senses, and now wild and fearful. What comes across is a sense
of desertion: the prisoner is left alone.

What this discussion suggests is that very often you can get
across the quality of a text by comparing it with something
which does not have quite the same quality. The comparison is
all the sharper if one cites as foil a text which is related; an influence, a source.

I cited, also in my second chapter, T. S. Eliot's poem 'Journey
of the Magi'. I cited it as an example of dramatic monologue;
I called attention to its 'touches of sharp detail'; I said that the
tone was that of a weary man who has suffered to the extreme of
his endurance. What I did not do was set by the side of the poem
the prose sermon that most certainly gave rise to it.

A cold comming they had of it, at this time of the yeare; just, the worst
time of the yeare, to take a journey, and specially a long journey, in.
The waies deep, the weather sharp, the daies short, the sunn farthest
off *in solstitio brumali,* the very dead of *Winter.*

This is Lancelot Andrewes's Sermon of the Nativity delivered at

Christmas in 1622. Lancelot Andrewes was a writer Eliot particularly admired. What he says of Andrewes's prose is also true
of his own verse adaptation. 'He slightly but sufficiently alters
the rhythm in proceeding more at large...[He] appears to
repeat, to stand still, but is nevertheless proceeding in the most
deliberate and orderly manner. There are often flashing phrases
which never desert the memory.' That 'alteration of the rhythm'
gave rise to the characteristic pattern of Eliot's verse in this
poem. Not 'they had a cold coming' but

> 'A cold coming we had of it,
> Just the worst time of the year
> For a journey, and such a long journey:
> The ways deep and the weather sharp,
> The very dead of winter...'

It is plain to see how this comparison can give rise to analysis;
an analysis that will show quite clearly the efficacy of Eliot's
verse. The narrative third person is put into a highly individual-
ized first person; the prose detail of 'worst time', 'long journey',
is backed up by the evocation of

> And the camels galled, sore-footed, refractory,
> Lying down in the melting snow...

It is as though hints in Lancelot Andrewes are developed in such
a way as to provide a highly distinctive atmosphere. Then we
can consider what, positively, Eliot has added. The evocation of
the luxuries the kings have left behind them, for instance –

> There were times we regretted
> The summer palaces on slopes, the terraces,
> And the silken girls bringing sherbet...

which acts as a contrast within the poem to another severe dose
of the journey –

> Then the camel men cursing and grumbling
> And running away, and wanting their liquor and women,
> And the night-fires going out, and the lack of shelters...

This is a kind of reference to and projection of various details
Andrewes mentions before the passage in his sermon that Eliot
actually uses: 'all the way wast and desolate', 'over the Rocks
and craggs of both Arabies'. Noting this will give you a chance
to point out that, in every instance, Eliot sharpens the details
and integrates them into his poem. The 'wast' is given to us in
particulars, and these particulars are part of the struggle to
reach the Christ-child. Even that struggle is not so bitter as the
sense of agony the three Kings feel at that birth. Once more, the
citation of a source is a way of bringing home to your reader the
quality of the finished product, the poem.

Sometimes the provenance of the finished work can be very
rich and suggestive indeed. There is a great deal behind the scene
from *Bleak House* which we looked at in Chapter 3. By bringing
Dickens's own writing into comparison with this background,
we can do something to demonstrate why his writing took the
shape that it did; more, we can demonstrate in what lies something of its efficacy.

The presiding idea is that of spontaneous combustion: the
idea that a person by ingesting spirits can set fire to himself in-
ternally and char to a heap of ash. Dickens had read, when he
was twelve, a horrific story reprinted from the *Gentleman's
Magazine* of 1746. It told of an old lady in the habit of consuming a great deal of wine and brandy who retired to bed and was
burned to ashes in the night by the action of the fiery evapor-
ations in her stomach. 'All the rest was ashes, which had this
quality, that they left in the hand a greasy and stinking moisture.
The air in the room had soot floating in it...the said soot flew
about, and from the lower part of the windows, trickled down a
greasy, loathsome yellowish liquor, with an unusual stink...'
This anecdote is reinforced with much supposedly historical circumstance, and was taken up, quite independently of Dickens,
by a number of other writers. Charles Brockden Brown in his
novel *Wieland* (1798) narrates how the hero's father is enveloped
by a fiery cloud which reduced his clothes to ashes and himself
to 'insupportable exhalations and crawling putrefaction'. Quite

likely this novel was known to Captain Marryat, who began his *Jacob Faithful* (1834) with the death of the hero's mother, an alcoholic, who retires to rest and who turns to smoke and ashes. In place of her body he finds 'a black mass in the centre of the bed. I put my hand fearfully upon it – it was a sort of unctuous, pitchy cinder'. Marryat explicitly tells us that the woman perished from spontaneous combustion, 'an inflammation of the gases generated from the spirits absorbed into the system'. Certainly *Jacob Faithful* would have been known to Herman Melville, another and far greater chronicler of the seas. In his novel *Redburn* (1849), Melville has a sailor in an alcoholic stupor emitting strange odours that combust when a light is held near his mouth – 'in a moment, the cadaverous face was crawled over by a swarm of wormlike flames'.

One reason for the extraordinary currency of this notion may have been fear, in the aftermath of the French Revolution, of further political activity. The image of spontaneous combustion furnished several writers with a convenient symbol for subversion. Coleridge, an essentially conservative writer, compares ignorance and superstition with a stifled and fermenting mass which, at the first admission of light and air, 'roars and blazes, and converts the already spoilt or damaged stuff with all the straw and straw-like matter near it, first into flame and the next moment into ashes' (*The Friend*, 1818). This image was taken up by Thomas Carlyle on several occasions. 'Let no man awaken it, this same Berserkir rage! Deep-hidden it lies, far down in the centre, like genial central-fire, with stratum after stratum of arrangement, traditionary method, composed productiveness, all built above it...' (*Chartism*, 1839). In the same work, Carlyle relates this subterranean rage to gin – 'liquid madness... If from this black unluminous unheeded *Inferno*, and Prisonhouse of souls in pain, there do flash up from time to time, some dismal wide-spread glare of Chartism or the like...are we to regard it as more baleful than the quiet state...?' Chartism, I should say, was a reform movement in the Britain of the 1830s and 1840s which worried many citizens because of its radical

tendency – a tendency to alter the existing system of society. It was,
not always fairly, associated with Luddism, or the wrecking of
factory machinery; also with incendiarism, particularly in the
form of rick-burning. Here is Carlyle again: 'These Twenty-four
million labouring men, if their affairs remain unregulated, chaotic, will burn ricks and mills; reduce us, themselves and the
world into ashes and ruin'. Benjamin Disraeli, novelist as well as
politician, shows the aristocrats ignoring this tendency in his
novel *Sybil* (1845).

'I wonder, talking of fires, that you are not more afraid of burning
ricks,' said Egremont.
   'It's an infernal lie,' said Lord Marney, very violently.
   'What is?' said Egremont.
   'That there is any incendiarism in this neighbourhood.'
   'Why there was a fire the day after I came.'
   'That had nothing to do with wages; it was an accident...'
   '...but no one has discovered the accident.'
   'For my part I believe it was spontaneous combustion,' said Lord
Marney.

The concept, so useful to political theorists, had its application even in the area of science. The great physicist, Michael
Faraday, used to give lectures for children at the Royal Institu-
tion. In one of these lectures, 'The Chemistry of a Candle', he
used the image of human digestion as an analogy for burning. 'It
is the combustion of the carbon by the contact of oxygen which
the body has supplied to it.' This was written up in a popular
form for Dickens's own journal, *Household Words*, and, in the
hands of the journalist doing the popularization, it acquired the
sensational aura of the anecdotage and fiction we have already
looked at. 'The charcoal goes entirely into carbonic acid gas,
and leaves nothing behind but ashes...a candle is a little gas
manufactory in itself, that burns the gas as fast as it makes
it...Breathing is consuming oxygen, only not so fast as burning...man is a candle, eh? and Shakespeare knew that...when
he wrote "Out, out, brief candle!"' (Charles Knight, *Household*

Words, 3 August 1850). It is the human more than the candle aspect of the matter that engages Dickens in *Bleak House;* and, as a radical, he applied the political connotations positively.

We can plainly see that what we have in the death of Krook is much more than the sum of a few anecdotes, a horrific novel or two, some interesting analogies in politics and in physical science. Spontaneous combustion is a powerful presence in *Bleak House,* and it is directed against the existing political system. The victims of law complain of injustice in its terms – 'it's being roasted at a slow fire' (Tom Jarndyce); 'I have been dragged for five-and-twenty years over burning iron' (Gridley). The court of Chancery is parodied by the old junk-merchant, Krook, with his shopful of papers and must and cobwebs. He is a highly distinctive figure: a stump of a man, frosted with white hairs, who breathes as though he were on fire within. This image is insisted upon throughout the book. Krook is 'a bundle of old clothes, with a spirituous heat smouldering in it'. Chancery is Krook on a monstrous scale, a gigantic funeral pyre. The mud of the earlier chapters metamorphoses into a dust that silts up the papers of the lawyers and settles like a rain of soot upon the ashes and broken bottles in the derelict shop of Lord Chancellor Krook. This is a remarkable example of an image existing at once as a fiction inside the novel and as a symbol outside it.

Krook's chancery is, like the body of its owner, a closed system, glutted, diseased and noxious. Krook soaks himself in gin until one evening he actually sets fire to his guts and explodes, so discharging his corrupt body into the atmosphere. It is an atmosphere built up by an accumulation of unwholesome particulars – vapour, soot, grease – that symbolically fuses together pestilence and law. The lawyer Weevle is under the illusion that he can trick Krook into letting him browse through secret documents; his friend Guppy believes this will lead them to uncover the heroine's identity and lead them to a great fortune. They wait for the Lord Chancellor – Krook, not Lord Lyndhurst – to unravel his mystery, but they might as well wait for the Court of Chancery to come to a conclusion. Weevle and Guppy descend

to Krook's parlour at the appointed time. But Krook has disin-
tegrated into bits and pieces, not immediately recognizable for
what they are. Yet, even in that state of disintegration, the corpse
retains a horrible likeness to what it was in life. As we saw in
Chapter 3, the withered body has become a charred log and its
white hairs are represented by white ashes. That seems actual
enough. On the symbolic plane, the death of Krook represents
the disintegration of Chancery, and, beyond Chancery, the
punishing and remorseless law of Dickens's society.

The Lord Chancellor of that Court, true to his title in his last act, has
died the death of all Lord Chancellors in all Courts, and of all authori-
ties in all places under all names soever, where false pretences are
made, and where injustice is done. Call the death by any name Your
Highness will, attribute it to whom you will, or say it might have been
prevented how you will, it is the same death eternally – inborn, inbred,
engendered in the corrupted humours of the vicious body itself, and
that only – Spontaneous Combustion, and none other of all the deaths
can be died.

It takes Dickens to portray, in the death of a gin-soaked old
man, the explosion of an entire legal system; indeed, implied
through that, a society. Yet even Dickens could not have done
this without the wealth of antecedent available to him. Nevertheless, it took an extraordinary imaginative technique to link up
tall stories, gothic novels, political images, scientific analogies
into a narrative that has far more point than any of its prece-
dents. The raw materials would have remained disparate but for
the great novelist's synthesizing hand whereby the literal and the
symbolic seem as one. Each detail, in other words, carries the
weight of several levels of meaning. Yet one does not experience
these levels separately. The technical term for this is synergy: the
whole is more than the sum of its parts.

However, we know that such spontaneous combustion cannot
take place: Dickens's dramatic fabric is based upon an impossi-
bility. Nevertheless, the narrative works: partly because the image symbolizes a basic human apprehension and partly because

of the accumulation of effect in a highly evocative prose –

a thick yellow liquor...a stagnant sickening oil...a little thick nauseous pool...a smouldering suffocating vapour in the room, and a
dark greasy coating on the walls and ceiling...the cinder of a small
charred and broken log of wood sprinkled with white ashes...

Undoubtedly the power is in the language. This can be
brought out by comparing this passage of *Bleak House* with its
antecedents. Locally, the distinction is between the 'greasy,
loathsome yellowish liquor' of Dickens's boyhood reading and
his own more concise rehandling, 'a thick yellow liquor'. It is the
difference between 'The floor of the chamber was thick smear'd
with a gluish moisture, not easily got off' and 'a dank greasy
coating on the walls and ceiling'. Dickens's 'coating' reminds us
of the greasy coat of Krook as he was in life, almost a part of his
anatomy, yet it leads us on to the tactile quality of the walls and
ceiling as though Krook had in death spread himself throughout
his environment. In Dickens, the implication is that Krook – not
some nameless substance – is not easily 'got off'! A great deal of
the effect in Dickens is his ability to evoke the man in death as he
was in his questionable life. More, he gives the distinct impression in his angling of the details that, if we ourselves do not
reform society, it is to this state it must eventually come. Partly
the effect is a matter of the building-up of tension; partly it is a
matter of rhythm and emphasis; partly, indeed, a judicious
admixture of comment amid the fiction: 'this...is all that represents him'.

The fiction of Dickens has a colour, odour and savour all of
its own, and it is more than the sum of its sources. We adduce
the sources in order to discuss the quality of the text. It is a text
that is at once clearly derivative and highly individual. This is by
no means a paradox unique among the great writers. One thinks
of the use Chaucer made of *novelle* from the French and Italian
languages, and of sermons and religious tracts; one thinks of the
advantage Shakespeare took of old plays, chronicles, Latin lyric

poetry, travellers' tales; of Joseph Conrad and his reworkings of anecdote, sailors' lore, hearsay, autobiographies, old newspapers. It is quite startlingly true of T. S. Eliot, as we have already seen; and we can take the matter on in the next chapter.

VIII Comparison and analysis

In the previous chapter my concerns may have looked historical, but in fact they were those which should engage the literary student. I adduced Ovid in the original and in Marlowe's translation to set off the quality of Wyatt's best poem; I adduced Lancelot Andrewes to show how an incisive prose could be adapted to bring new rhythms into verse; and I also tried to show how the imagery of minor novelists like Brockden Brown and Marryat and of major social critics like Coleridge and Carlyle could receive a decisive rehandling by Dickens in *Bleak House*. This is not to discount the virtue of source-hunting or the relevance of citing analogues. But, unless comparison enhances our appreciation of the literary text centrally under discussion, such background work is a branch of history. It may very well be a branch worth study in itself, but from our point of view as literary students its main function is to inform criticism.

This can be attempted in a way less sternly evaluative than was the case in the last chapter. I hope there I said enough to indicate that *Bleak House* is a very great work indeed; but its greatness, of course, does not prevent its being, in its turn, an influence. Its very richness of texture has enabled it to serve as matrix from which a number of writings have been stamped out. Some of these are attractive but distinctively minor, like the stories of Conan Doyle; some are remarkably different from their source of origin, yet clearly owe allegiance to it.

It is the more direct narrative of *Bleak House* that is behind the texts we are to look at. This, for instance:

Fog everywhere. Fog up the river, where it flows among green aits and meadows; fog down the river, where it rolls defiled among the tiers of shipping, and the waterside pollutions of a great (and dirty) city. Fog on the Essex marshes, fog on the Kentish heights. Fog creeping into the cabooses of collier-brigs; fog lying out on the yards, and hovering in the rigging of great ships; fog drooping on the gunwales of barges and small boats. Fog in the eyes and throats of ancient Greenwich pensioners, wheezing by the firesides of their wards; fog in the stem and bowl of the afternoon pipe of the wrathful skipper, down in his close cabin; fog cruelly pinching the toes and fingers of his shivering little 'prentice boy on deck. Chance people on the bridges peeping over the parapets into a nether sky of fog, with fog all round them, as if they were up in a balloon, and hanging in the misty clouds...

I am not going to say that Dickens was the first author to insist on fog as a physical presence. There are antecedents in two writers who influenced him greatly, Thomas De Quincey and Leigh Hunt; and the syntactical pattern of insistence here derives from Leigh Hunt's essays. But the extended tactile qualities Dickens gives to the fog, the animal application of 'fog creeping...fog lying...hovering...drooping...' – that, indeed, is Dickens's own. It gave a definite direction to the way in which subsequent authors dealt with the phenomenon:

'Stand at the window here. Was there ever such a dreary, dismal, unprofitable world? See how the yellow fog swirls down the street and drifts across the dun-coloured houses...'

(The Sign of Four)

A thick fog rolled down between the lines of dun-coloured houses, and the opposing windows loomed like dark, shapeless blurs, through the heavy yellow wreaths. Our gas was lit, and shone on the white cloth, and glimmer of china and metal...

('The Copper Beeches')

In the third week of November, in the year 1895, a dense yellow fog settled down upon London...after pushing back our chairs from breakfast we saw the greasy, heavy brown swirl still drifting past us and condensing in oily drops upon the window-panes...

('The Adventure of the Bruce-Partington Plans')

These are snippets from Conan Doyle's Sherlock Holmes stories, and I could easily double and redouble the instances. Part of their undeniable charm is the imaginative use of Dickens. Of course there *was* fog in London, and plenty of people noticed it, but this is a particular mode of vision. The fog, as with Dickens, is curiously alive – it swirls, it drifts, it rolls, settles, drifts again and condenses in oily drops upon the window-panes. Further, it gives rise to this –

> The yellow fog that rubs its back upon the window-panes,
> The yellow smoke that rubs its muzzle on the window-panes
> Licked its tongue into the corners of the evening,
> Lingered upon the pools that stand in drains,
> Let fall upon its back the soot that falls from chimneys,
> Slipped by the terrace, made a sudden leap,
> And seeing that it was a soft October night,
> Curled once about the house, and fell asleep.

> And indeed there will be time
> For the yellow smoke that slides along the street
> Rubbing its back upon the window-panes;
> There will be time, there will be time
> To prepare a face to meet the faces that you meet;
> There will be time to murder and create,
> And time for all the works and days of hands
> That lift and drop a question on your plate;
> Time for you and time for me,
> And time yet for a hundred indecisions,
> And for a hundred visions and revisions,
> Before the taking of a toast and tea. ...

('The Love Song of J. Alfred Prufrock')

It is interesting that T. S. Eliot had to go to Conan Doyle as an intermediary between himself and Dickens. Conan Doyle has this odd distinction: that, though a devotee of Dickens, his work is not eccentrically Dickensian. Many of Dickens's imitators pick up only the mannerisms of the great man: they cough like Dickens, so to speak, and like him are short. The Inimitable Boz, as he liked to call himself, was no easy influence to assimilate. Yet, in Conan Doyle, influence from a number of areas in Dickens's output was picked up and reshaped into a distinctive texture. The partnership of an alert intelligence with one that is prosaic, which we associate with Sherlock Holmes and Dr Watson, may have been most immediately suggested by Eugene Wrayburn and Mortimer Lightwood, the inseparable companions of *Our Mutual Friend*; Dickens's interest in crime is not necessarily associated with fog, in *Bleak House* or elsewhere, but the association is made obsessively in Conan Doyle. Therefore it is no wonder that Eliot, in his turn, moves from the highly imaginative evocation of the fog in such stories as 'The Copper Beeches' and 'The Adventure of the Bruce-Partington Plans' to 'There will be time to murder and create' and the recollection of the breakfast scene that so often acts as a contrast to the fog in the Sherlock Holmes stories – 'a hundred visions and revisions / Before the taking of a toast and tea'.

We can use Conan Doyle as a foil for comparison in this matter of the fog. It does not have, in his work, the inclusive humanity of Dickens, with his wrathful skipper and shivering 'prentice boy. Nor does it have the convoluting life manifested in Eliot. Nevertheless, Conan Doyle enabled Eliot to import into his verse something of the monstrous character of Krook's end which is part of the less direct narrative mode in *Bleak House*. Eliot's fog is not content to stay outside the windows: it seems about to effect an entry into the room. It does not just swirl round the house: it curls round it, rubbing alternately its back and its muzzle quite horribly against the window panes. It licks its tongue into quite unspeakable corners of the evening. It has a dramatic function in the story as, for all its qualities, the 'Baker Street particular' in Sherlock Holmes has not.

The comparison helps us to look at the texture of Eliot's verse more closely. In Eliot, the fog is a monstrous cat, sliding around insidiously but capable of a sudden and terrible leap. No better evocation has come my way of the sinister qualities of feline life; perhaps no better evocation of fog.

The matter does not stop there. The fog itself wreathes round the life of Eliot's frustrated hero, the timorous Alfred Prufrock. The fog is representative of the urban life that blots from him the sources of vitality. He is pinned down by eyes that fix him in a familiar phrase. On a good day he may get out to paddle on the beach. But he is cut off from what, on a good day, he can glimpse: the mermaids –

> I have seen them riding seaward on the waves
> Combing the white hair of the waves blown back
> When the wind blows the water white and black...

This evocation of freedom and energy gives us a sense of context and a plangency which we do not find in Conan Doyle. We do not find, it seems to me, the more positive aspects displayed here even in Dickens.

Yet 'Prufrock', like a good deal of Eliot's early writing, was quite original enough to cause utter consternation among the critics. It is by an act of historical imagination that we get a sense of these poems being hotly advocated by Ezra Pound, I. A. Richards, F. R. Leavis; advocated, moreover, against a tide of incredulity and even contempt. George Gordon, Merton Professor of English Literature at Oxford, expressed what may be taken to be an official view in his inaugural lecture in 1934. Speaking of Eliot, he says 'Over his London – for he is a town-poet, and London is his dejected citadel – there hangs perpetual fog through which we are conducted with fastidious dandyism past all the staleness of its muddled and crowded life...We are in danger of arriving at a kind of code or shorthand poetry, built on allusion, and written by specialists for specialists...' After that, we hardly need to quote Sir John Squire's response to 'The Waste Land' – 'a grunt would serve equally well' (*London Mer-*

cury, 1922). Such critics failed in the most crucial task a critic can undertake: holding the pass against the inertness of academic opinion, recognizing the genuinely new writer at the time of his writing. Being genuinely new need not, as we have seen, involve a rootless modernity. Too often the Bad Critics resist the great author of their time because they have forgotten the live tradition in which such an author necessarily works.

Tradition, as I insisted in my book *Tradition and Experiment,* is no mere copying of existing mannerisms. It is rather a creative use of past writing in an effort to make something live. The technique of comparison and analysis which I am seeking to demonstrate here is one way of recognizing this. For exámple, there is no more creative use of sources than that which you will find in Jane Austen. We saw in Chapter 3 how she deployed a mode of distancing; in Chapter 5 we looked at the way in which she structured *Pride and Prejudice,* through key scenes. Now let us consider how she refined the frequently crude usages of her predecessors into literature.

The distancing mode characteristic of Jane Austen I called low-mimetic, meaning that we were not encouraged to throw ourselves into the action and to identify with the central character. In Chapter 3 I suggested that Samuel Richardson and Fanny Burney were, so to speak, Jane Austen's neighbours in that mode; but it was not my brief, at that juncture, to discuss the use she made of them. Then I was concerned with similarities; but now I am concerned with contrast.

This is because, it has to be said, often a good writer draws upon material that is manifestly inferior. The supreme source-book for Jane Austen was not, as might have been expected, the great classic, *Clarissa;* it was Richardson's later, and much less readable book, *Sir Charles Grandison.* This must not be underestimated as a force in its time: it was an attempt to put forward an ideal of civilization embodied in a perfect English gentleman; and it was read all over Europe. But its interest for us now is largely historical, and I shall have no qualms about using it as a means of showing how its relative crudity was refined, through the intermediary work of Fanny Burney, into the characteristic precision of Jane Austen's comedy.

Harriet Byron has been abducted by the evil Sir Hargrave Pollexfen, a counterbalance in the novel for the perfect Grandison. She is carried off from a fashionable ball by a substitute sedan chair with substitute chairmen. She finds herself being importuned by Pollexfen in the home of a widow he has misled as to their relationship.

The vile wretch entered. I left her, and kneeled to him. I knew not what I did. I remember I said, wringing my hands, 'If you have mercy; if you have compassion, let me now, now, I beseech you, sir, this moment, experience your mercy.' He gave them some motion, I suppose to withdraw, for by that time the widow and the other daughter were in the parlour, and they all retired.

'I have besought *you,* madam, and on my *knees* too, to show *me* mercy; but none would you show me, inexorable Miss Byron! Kneel, if you will; in your turn kneel, supplicate, pray; you cannot be more in earnest than I was. Now are the tables turned.'

'Barbarous man!' said I, rising from my knees. My spirit was raised, but it as instantly subsided. 'Be not, I beseech you, Sir Hargrave, cruel to me. I never was cruel to anybody. You know I was civil to you; I was *very* civil –'

'Yes, yes, and very determined. You called me no names. I call you none, Miss Byron. You were very civil. Hitherto *I* have not been uncivil. But remember, madam – But, sweet, and ever-adorable creature,' and he clasped his arms about me; 'your very terror is beautiful! I can *enjoy* your terror, madam.' And the savage would have kissed me. My averted head frustrated his intention; and at his feet I besought him not to treat the poor creature, whom he had so vilely betrayed, with indignity.

'*I don't hit your fancy, madam!*'

'Can you be a malicious man, Sir Hargrave?'

'*You don't like my morals, madam!*'

'And is this the way, Sir Hargrave, are these the means you take to convince me that I ought to like them?'

'Well, madam, you shall prove the mercy in me you would not show. You shall see that I cannot be a malicious man; a revengeful man; and yet you have raised my pride. You shall find me a *moral* man.'

'Then, Sir Hargrave, will I bless you from the bottom of my heart!'

'But you know what will justify me in every eye for the steps I have taken. Be mine, madam: be legally mine. I offer you my honest hand. Consent to be Lady Pollexfen.'

'What, sir! justify by so poor, so very poor, a compliance, steps that you have so basely taken! Take my life, sir! But my hand and my heart are my own: they never shall be separated.' I arose from my knees, trembling, and threw myself upon the window-seat, and wept bitterly. He came to me. I looked on this side, and on that, wishing to avoid him.

What is worrying in this prose is the way in which the violent action fails to be contained by the narrative. It is an example of the fallacy of imitative form; naturalism gone wrong. The narrative is too near that which it narrates. Richardson has violated his own low-mimetic mode, and done so to no effect. A phrase like 'vile wretch' names, but does not display, the wretch's vileness. In life, a girl in this situation might very well make violent gestures, yet 'wringing my hands' is a phrase too well-worn to do more than state a probability. This is not so much an imitation of life as a recollection of stage melodrama: '"Barbarous man!" said I, rising from my knees'; 'my averted head frustrated his intention'; 'the poor creature, whom he had so vilely betrayed' – the emotion is stated, in these imprecise terms; it is not acted out as significant narrative.

But even what I have said is statement, not over-precise; and it can perhaps be made precise only by means of comparison. This crude aspect of Richardson was, as I have said, influential, and we shall now see Fanny Burney trying to make use of it. Pollexfen's attempt at abduction is, in *Evelina,* geared down to a strategem on the part of an unwelcome suitor to secure a private interview. As with Richardson, so here: there is a close association of private interview with means of transport. In this case, Sir Clement escorts Evelina to his carriage and prolongs the journey by instructing his coachman to go the wrong way.

I courtsied my thanks. Sir Clement, with great earnestness, pressed me to go; and while I was thus uneasily deliberating what to do, the dance, I suppose, finished, for the people crowded down stairs. Had Lord Orville then repeated his offer, I would have accepted it notwithstanding Sir Clement's repugnance; but I fancy he thought it would be impertinent. In a very few minutes I heard Madame Duval's voice, as she descended from the gallery. 'Well,' cried I hastily, 'if I must go –' I stopt; but Sir Clement immediately handed me into his chariot, called out, 'Queen Ann Street,' and then jumped in himself. Lord Orville, with a bow and a half smile, wished me good night.

My concern was so great at being seen and left by Lord Orville in so strange a situation, that I should have been best pleased to have remained wholly silent during our ride home; but Sir Clement took care to prevent that.

He began by making many complaints of my unwillingness to trust myself with him, and begged to know what could be the reason? This question so much embarrassed me, that I could not tell what to answer; but only said, that I was sorry to have taken up so much of his time.

'O Miss Anville,' cried he, taking my hand, 'if you knew with what transport I would dedicate to you not only the present but all the future time allotted to me, you would not injure me by making such an apology.'

I could not think of a word to say to this, nor to a great many other equally fine speeches with which he ran on; though I would fain have withdrawn my hand, and made almost continual attempts; but in vain, for he actually grasped it between both his, without any regard to my resistance.

Soon after, he said that he believed the coachman was going the wrong way; and he called to his servant, and gave him directions. Then again addressing himself to me, 'How often, how assiduously have I sought an opportunity of speaking to you, without the presence of that brute, Captain Mirvan! Fortune has now kindly favoured me with one; and permit me,' again seizing my hand, 'permit me to use it in telling you that I adore you.'

I was quite thunderstruck at this abrupt and unexpected declaration. For some moments I was silent; but when I recovered from my surprise, I said, 'Indeed, Sir, if you were determined to make me repent leaving my own party so foolishly, you have very well succeeded.'

We may not be disturbed by the crudities so evident in the texture of *Sir Charles Grandison,* but it is impossible to remain at ease with this style. I think it is a matter of instability in tone: Fanny Burney has adapted the Richardson mode by importing into it a number of comic effects, yet the overall effect is not that of comedy. It would not be simplifying our criticism too much to say that we cannot tell how funny *Evelina* is trying to be. The novel is full of sudden, rather fussy, movements: 'I courtsied my thanks', 'Sir Clement...pressed me to go', 'the people crowded down stairs', 'Sir Clement immediately handed me into his chariot...and then jumped in himself'. Instead of Pollexfen's rude attempt to kiss the heroine, Fanny Burney has Sir Clement seize Evelina by the hand; instead of ruffianly sneers and threats, we have Sir Clement's asseverations; where Harriet Byron 'wept bitterly', Evelina is 'quite thunderstruck'. The melodrama has been toned down to an element of horseplay, but this is not quite assimilated. It is not helped by an overlooking presence, an authorial self, not absorbed into the first-person narrative. The effect is that of self-consciousness – 'I was silent...I recovered... I said'. The 'I' attracts the wrong sort of attention and interposes itself between reader and narrative.

Yet this, and the Richardsonian element of violence, is absorbed into the texture of *Emma* and thoroughly utilized. We have the sense of quick action, but the quickness is in aid of comedy. There is a sense of affront on the part of the young lady, but we ourselves do not have to share it: the reader is conscious, as the heroine is not, of the absurdity of the scene. Emma has been seeking to recommend her dull little friend Harriet Smith to the attention of the handsome young vicar, and the result is that he mistakes her intentions and supposes them to be directed towards himself.

Isabella stept in after her father; John Knightley, forgetting that he did not belong to their party, stept in after his wife very naturally; so that Emma found, on being escorted and followed into the second carriage by Mr Elton, that the door was to be lawfully shut on them, and that they were to have a *tête-à-tête* drive. It would not have been the awkwardness of a moment, it would have been rather a pleasure previous to the suspicions of this very day; she would have talked to him of Harriet, and the three quarters of a mile would have seemed but one. But now, she would rather it had not happened. She believed he had been drinking too much of Mr Weston's good wine, and felt sure that he would want to be talking nonsense.

To restrain him as much as might be, by her own manners she was immediately preparing to speak with exquisite calmness and gravity of the weather and the night; but scarcely had she begun, scarcely had they passed the sweep-gate and joined the other carriage, than she found her subject cut up – her hand seized – her attention demanded, and Mr Elton actually making violent love to her: availing himself of the precious opportunity, declaring sentiments which must be already well known, hoping – fearing – adoring – ready to die if she refused him; but flattering himself that his ardent attachment and unequalled love and unexampled passion could not fail of having some effect, and, in short, very much resolved on being seriously accepted as soon as possible. It really was so. Without scruple – without apology – without much apparent diffidence, Mr Elton, the lover of Harriet, was professing himself *her* lover. She tried to stop him; but vainly; he would go on, and say it all. Angry as she was, the thought of the moment made her resolve to restrain herself when she did speak. She felt that half this folly must be drunkenness, and therefore could hope that it might belong only to the passing hour. Accordingly, with a mixture of the serious and the playful, which she hoped would best suit his half and half state, she replied—

'I am very much astonished, Mr Elton. This to *me*, you forget yourself – you take me for my friend – any message to Miss Smith I shall be happy to deliver; but no more of this to *me*, if you please.'

'Miss Smith! – Message to Miss Smith! – What could she possibly mean!' – And he repeated her words with such assurance of accent, such boastful pretence of amazement, that she could not help replying with quickness –

'Mr Elton, this is the most extraordinary conduct! and I can account for it only in one way; you are not yourself, or you could not

speak either to me, or of Harriet, in such a manner. Command yourself
enough to say no more, and I will endeavour to forget it.'

Jane Austen, here as elsewhere, uses as a technique of comedy
the contrast between how people see themselves and how they
may seem to the reader. It is more complex than the proposal of
Mr Collins in *Pride and Prejudice*; here, both participants in the
dialogue make fools of themselves. The technique is worthy of
remark: a phrase like 'she was immediately preparing to speak
with exquisite calmness and gravity' carries some odd overtones.
This is Emma talking, not the author: it would seèm more appropriate to Emma's way of seeing herself than to our way of seeing her; it is that word 'exquisite' that gives the clue. In any case,
she is never given the chance to proceed. Like the heroine of
Evelina, Emma finds that her hand is seized, and the seizure bor-
ders not on violence but on incongruity. This incongruity at once
points the comedy and keeps at bay the sentimentality which
is never far away in *Evelina*. So confident is Jane Austen of her
tone that she speaks of Mr Elton as actually making 'violent
love'. It is a calculated over-statement. In fact the 'violent love'
manifests itself as a torrent of sentiments relayed to us through
the ironically detached sensibility of the author. The words are
those of sentimental theatre, but they are so copious, so broken
up and so encapsulated by the surrounding irony, as to have the
effect of at once seeming familiar and being absurd – 'hoping
– fearing – adoring – ready to die if she refused him; but flattering himself that his ardent attachment and unequalled love and
unexampled passion could not fail of having some effect...' Indirect speech, of which this is a fine example, is a precarious
technique: there is always the possibility of a hiatus between the
force of the sentiments and the manner of their relay. Jane Austen is not only aware of the hiatus; she utilizes it. It is a dramatiz-
ation of the gap between what Elton thinks he is doing and what
we – through the eyes of the author – see actually done.

A technique not wholly dissimilar is used with regard to Emma
herself. In a Victorian novel a heroine might well express herself

in the tones of a Lord Chief Justice pronouncing from on high; and the author might well be behind her. But Jane Austen was no Victorian. Emma's eloquence is unsupported by any authorial warrant and consequently sounds pompous. '"Command yourself enough to say no more"' out of context sounds like a line of blank verse from a heroic tragedy and in context sounds like Emma fooling herself at the same time as she unintentionally makes a fool of Mr Elton.

Jane Austen's prose, as all this will show, bears a degree of analysis hardly equalled by that of any other author. It is because of dexterity and variegation of nuance that she remains almost indefinitely re-readable. What is functionless incongruity in other works becomes, with Jane Austen, a mode of comedy. But I doubt whether the point could be made so firmly if one did not have *Evelina* and *Sir Charles Grandison* to draw upon as foils. Comparison is a sound foundation for analysis: one does not only describe that which one believes to be excellent but also calls upon contrast from works that are manifestly inferior in order to reinforce the valuation.

Comparison is not always so straightforward as this. One could point to a different sort of contrast between *Recollections of the Lake Poets* (1834–40) by Thomas De Quincey and *The Spirit of the Age* (1825) by William Hazlitt. These are two books very much of their period, a mixture of criticism and biography, often dealing with what seem to be the same topics. Yet De Quincey remembers Wordsworth in one way, and Hazlitt in another, and there is no method of settling the differential between them. It is quite likely that the reader will prefer one to the other, but it would be difficult to state the preference in critical terms. De Quincey is unendingly garrulous, but full of insight and incident as he rambles on. Hazlitt is far more purged and prosaic, very much a man talking to men, but somehow lacking in the quality of vision that intermittently illumines De Quincey. De Quincey describes Wordsworth by comparing him with Scott and throwing a piercing side-glance at the head of Charles Lamb – 'absolutely truncated in the posterior region – sawn off, as it were, by no timid sawyer'. Hazlitt sees Wordsworth in terms of a Holbein portrait 'grave, saturnine, with a slight indication of sly humour, kept under by the manners of the age or by the pretensions of the person'. De Quincey moves from description of physical semblance to interpretation; often in fantastic, if not extravagant, terms –

Neither are the eyes of Wordsworth 'large', as is erroneously stated somewhere in 'Peter's Letters'; on the contrary, they are (I think) rather small; but *that* does not interfere with their effect, which at times is fine and suitable to his intellectual character. At times, I say, for the depth and subtlety of eyes varies exceedingly with the state of the stomach; and, if young ladies were aware of the magical transformations which can be wrought in the depth and sweetness of the eye by a few weeks' walking exercise, I fancy we should see their habits in this point altered greatly for the better. I have seen Wordsworth's eyes oftentimes affected powerfully in this respect; his eyes are not, under any circumstances, bright, lustrous, or piercing; but, after a long day's toil in walking, I have seen them assume an appearance the most solemn and spiritual that it is possible for the human eye to wear. The light which resides in them is at no time a superficial light; but, under favourable accidents, it is a light which seems to come from depths below all depths; in fact, it is more truly entitled to be held 'The light that never was on land or sea', a light radiating from some far spiritual world, than any the most idealizing light that ever a painter's hand created.

The tone is that of the inspired gossip, the raconteur, the biographer.

The tone of Hazlitt, on the other hand, is that of the critic. He anchors his remarks on Wordsworth's appearance very much to the great writer reading his own poetry, and in the end it is the poetry that is the object of his attention –

He has a peculiar sweetness in his smile, and great depth and manliness and a rugged harmony, in the tones of his voice. His manner of reading his own poetry is particularly imposing; and in his favourite passages his eye beams with preternatural lustre, and the meaning labours slowly up from his swelling breast. No one who has seen him at these moments could go away with an impression that he was a 'man of no mark or likelihood'. Perhaps the comment of his face and voice is necessary to convey a full idea of his poetry. His language may not be intelligible, but his manner is not to be mistaken. It is clear that he is either mad or inspired.

This comparison may serve to remind us that the discussion of literature is not always a matter of 'either/or'. We are lucky to have the prose of both De Quincey and Hazlitt. The qualities of the one are not the qualities of the other; indeed, it is remarkable to consider that, at a given period, a given language could produce writers, ostensibly utilizing the same form, so utterly contrasting.

Comparisons can take us along this line of argument further even than that. Suppose one had a writer who was wedded to detail; scrupulously honest, but incontestably dull. Suppose, in contrast, there was a writer treating the same subject but angling its detail, and even distorting it, to produce a caricature whose traits were dubiously recognizable. Some kind of preference ought to be indicated here, but it is no easy matter to say quite what it should be.

My case is not hypothetical. I would like you to consider the two passages following. Both are about Florence Nightingale who supervised nursing services in the Crimean War and who is usually thought to be the founder of nursing as a profession. The first passage is an extract from her official biography, published by the sometime editor of the *Daily News* in 1913.

It is a natural temptation of biographers to give a formal unity to their subject by representing the child as in all things the father of the man; to date the vocation of their hero or heroine very early in life; to magnify some childish incident as prophetic of what is to come thereafter. Material is available for such treatment in the case of Florence Nightingale. It has been recorded that she used to nurse and bandage dolls which her elder sister damaged. Every book about the heroine of the Crimea contains, too, a tale of 'first aid to the wounded' which Florence administered to Cap, the Shepherd's collie, whom she found with a broken leg on the downs near Embley. 'I wonder,' wrote her 'old Pastor'[1] to her in 1858, 'whether you remember how, twenty-two years ago, you and I together averted the intended hanging of poor old Shepherd Smither's dog, Cap. How many times I have told the story since! I well recollect the pleasure which the saving of the life of a poor dog then gave to your young mind. I was delighted to witness it; it was to me not indeed an omen of what you were about to do and be (for of that I never dreamed), but it was an index of that kind and benevolent disposition, of that I Cor. xiii. Charity, which has been at the root of it.' And it is certainly interesting and curious, if nothing more, that the very earliest piece in the handwriting of Florence Nightingale which has been preserved should be a medical prescription. It is contained in a tiny book, about the size of a postage stamp, which the little girl stiched together and in which the instruction is written, in very childish letters, '16 grains for an old woman, 11 for a young woman, and 7 for a child'. But these things are after all but trifles. Florence Nightingale is not the only little girl who has been fond of nursing sick dolls or mending them when broken. Other children have tended wounded animals and had their pill-boxes and simples.

SIR EDWARD COOK

The second extract is from *Eminent Victorians* (1918) by Lytton Strachey, critic, historian and star of the Bloomsbury Group.

Ah! To do her duty in that state of life unto which it had pleased God to call her! Assuredly she would not be behindhand in doing her duty; but unto what state of life had it pleased Him to call Charlotte Corday, or Elizabeth of Hungary? What was that secret voice in her ear, if it was not a call? Why had she felt, from her earliest years, those mysterious promptings towards...she hardly knew what, but certainly towards something very different around her? Why, as a child in the nursery, when her sister had shown a healthy pleasure in tearing her dolls to pieces, had she shown an almost morbid one in sewing them up again? Why was she driven now to minister to the poor in the cottages, to watch by sick-beds, to put her dog's wounded paw into elaborate splints as if it was a human being? Why was her head filled with queer

[1] The Rev. J. T. Gifford

imaginations of the country house at Embley turned, by some enchant-
ment into a hospital, with herself as matron moving about among the
beds? Why was even her vision of heaven itself filled with suffering
patients to whom she was being useful? So she dreamed and wondered,
and, taking out her diary, she poured into it the agitations of her soul.
And then the bell rang, and it was time to go and dress for dinner.

LYTTON STRACHEY

No one can fail to find the first passage less intrinsically interesting than the second. The style is plodding: 'It is a natural
temptation...'; 'Material is available...'; 'It has been recorded' – there is a heavy dependence on the passive voice and the
verb 'to be'. This goes along with an avoidance of sensationalism. Wisely, but not captivatingly, Sir Edward Cook declares
that many young children play at nurse with dolls but only one
of them became Florence Nightingale.

In contrast, Lytton Strachey's sparkling style goes with the
positive embracement of sensationalism. 'Ah! To do her
duty...What was that secret voice in her ear...? why had she
felt, from her earliest years, those mysterious promptings...?'
Not only does Lytton Strachey proclaim Florence Nightingale's
trafficking with the sick-bed to be exceptional to herself but he
pronounces it morbid. It is all part of a debunking of Florence
Nightingale as a Victorian heroine in particular, and the Victorians in general.

Here, and elsewhere, Lytton Strachey is not particular about
fact if he can angle it in the direction of sensationalism. His is
the mind of the so-called investigative journalist: it is not that of
the respectable critic or historian! In the official life of another
Victorian worthy, it is recorded that Cardinal Manning, then a
Protestant clergyman, made no entry in his diary about his meeting with Pope Pius IX in 1848. This lacuna Lytton Strachey
turns into a 'fact'. In the absence of any statement by which he
could be confuted, the author of *Eminent Victorians* invents
wildly. 'What did Pio Nono say? It is easy to imagine the persuasive innocence of his Italian voice "Ah, dear Signor Manning,

why don't you come over to us? Do you suppose that we should not look after you?"' I could give kindred instances from Strachey's 'lives' of his other Eminent Victorians: Dr Arnold, General Gordon, Queen Victoria herself.

No one could call Strachey dull; merely inaccurate. Even this would not matter if he did not purport to be presenting history. Admittedly history, like criticism itself, is based on selection; but it is impermissible to fill up the absence of fact with inference, and to flesh out facts that are tenuous with wild imagining. The equivalent in criticism would be reading into an unsatisfactory text one's private fantasies. Lytton Strachey has fallen between two areas of writing. It is interesting to consider what would have been the difference of effect if he had presented his facts as fiction. He could have written stories loosely based upon the lives of the Victorians yet not explicitly presenting themselves as biography. Then we should have had something like the following –

Why, as a child in the nursery, when her sister had shown a healthy pleasure in tearing her dolls to pieces, had Jennie Linnet shown an almost morbid one in sewing them up again...?

(Jennie Linnet, Nursing Sister)

...What did Hadrian VIII say? It is easy to imagine the persuasive innocence of his Italian voice 'Ah, dear Canon Bonynge, why don't you come over to us? Do you suppose that we should not look after you...?'

(Over to Rome: an Ecclesiastical Romance)

We can accept as fiction what we know to be founded on fact, even if the fact can be somewhat distorted. It is the names in Strachey that throw us off balance because they bring us up against other areas of information, some of which relate to knowledge we already have and which therefore seem preferable. The fictionalized 'Florence Nightingale' or 'Cardinal Manning' that Strachey puts forward jostle uneasily against their historical prototypes.

The difficulty is even greater when the fiction is presented not only as though it was fact, but wittily; while the history, as honest history sometimes tends to be, is dull. A trenchant modern instance can be found in the brilliant cinematography of Ken Russell. I found his film *The Music Lovers* an absorbing experience, but he should not have called his central character Tchaikovsky.

What I have done here is to use analytical comparison to demonstrate not only a critical point but an aesthetic one. We have entered literary theory. However, whether one is aware of it or not, there is an implied theory in any and every critical statement. Nowadays it is best expressed by urging the reader to be aware of his standpoint. I am conscious, in writing here, of using a prose derived, at however many removes, from Bertrand Russell and Yvor Winters. My attitude towards literature relates to that of T. S. Eliot and F. R. Leavis; the latter, in fact, was my teacher. This means, of course, that my own approach to literature is angled. No doubt a technical Marxist or a doctrinaire Freudian would approach a text in a different way. This could be a falsification if, say, the Marxist were to blame Jane Austen for failing to describe the labouring poor of Longbourn or Highbury in terms of the class struggle. Any such approach would be to ignore what Jane Austen offers in favour of something that she does not. In effect, it would be to substitute for the text a fantasy. Yet there have been Marxist critics who put their characteristic standpoint to good use: Marx himself on *Timon of Athens,* Lenin on Tolstoy, Trotsky on Formalist Criticism – to come no nearer to our own time. Much, no doubt, depends on the text chosen for comment; much depends on its relationship with the critic choosing to discuss it.

As I said in Chapter 1, what we are doing in criticism is arguing a case. It would not do to suppose that any one critic has a key to the Eternal Verities. Rather, what he says has to be appropriate to his circumstances, appropriate to the text – and appropriate to the reader, too. We must recognize in that sentence how great a weight is put on the term 'appropriate'. It can only be made functional by particularizing more closely, and saying that in the present instance I am a teacher of literature addressing himself to students in the context of a university. This involves the implicit taking up of certain assumptions; such as my readers believing in the utility of literature and wishing themselves to gain some proficiency in writing about it. My words would fail to persuade a general in El Salvador, a Yahoo from the land of the Houyhnhnms, very small children, or visitors from Alpha Centauri. Clearly, then, there is a presumed relationship between text and reader, and between the reader, when that reader is a critic writing for publication, and a presumed audience. But this need not, as I hope to show in the next chapter, lead us to absolutism.

IX The model essay/Breaking the model

From what I have said you may think that I have an ideal essay in mind to which all future essays must conform. This is not so. Nevertheless, I would advocate the following techniques as being among the desirable methods to follow.

(1) When faced with a task, whether it be a tutorial essay or an examination paper, assemble your materials – texts, critical adjuncts, notes – well in advance. Try to commit some portions of your text to memory.

(2) If you are writing a tutorial essay on a given topic, be sure to answer the question that has been put to you and do not wander off into irrelevance.

(3) What I have said under (2) also applies to examination papers. In addition, remember that timing is essential. It is no use writing a copious first answer, followed by a sketchy second answer and concluding with an unfinished scrap. If three answers are called for, timetable the paper in such a way as to fulfil this requirement. If you find timetabling difficult, write practice answers under examination conditions in your own time.

(4) Write three or four notes before you begin an answer or an essay. Label them in such a way as to suggest a sequence of ideas. If any one note does not fit it, cancel it before you start writing extensively.

(5) Whether in or out of the examination room, address yourself to particulars. Try to back up each statement with a quotation (or detailed reference) and each quotation (or detailed reference) with some show of analysis.

(6) Endeavour to write a lucid prose. Especially make sure that every sentence has a clearly determinable subject.

(7) Try to write persuasively. In particular, make sure that you begin and end strongly.

Now, at first sight, this may seem highly prescriptive. But if you ask a person, as I do in (4) above, to structure an essay, you are not necessarily imposing a structure on that person. The essay could focus on one particular scene of a play and build a context of argument involving other aspects of the play around it. It could take a play and hunt a particular image or image sequence through it. The essay could take a character and analyse that character in terms of its function in the total drama. Other possibilities include problems of dramaturgy, or the relationship of the various sources with the finished work. When I speak of structure, then, I do not mean to say that only one structure is possible. What I think, however, is that to a great extent structure is determined by the subject prescribed for an essay or the question asked in an examination paper. It is no good the student discussing the symbolism of *Othello* if he has been asked to gauge in terms of dramatic effect the machinations of Iago.

Many will feel that such an approach narrows down the possibilities of a critique. It does: criticism, as I have said, is a craft of selection. It is my view that many critical essays suffer because they extrapolate from a text or ramble around it rather than focus on any particular aspect. However, there are ways of dealing with this problem, as with others. If you are writing about a specific poet, clearly you cannot cover all of his output. You will have to concentrate on three or four of the poems in depth. Which ones they are will be to some degree dependent upon the question you have been asked. However, it is possible to bring in other poems treated glancingly, either as foils for comparison or as bridges from one part of the argument to the next. This is one of several techniques that can be deployed to give the impression of windows opening out of what might otherwise seem a restricted line of argument.

Similarly: I recommended, in (6) above, that a student should do his best to write a lucid prose. But I also intimated, in Chapter 4, that several modes of prose were possible. It is true that I expressed my own preference for the mode of the Expositor: the kind of prose I associate with such writers as Bertrand Russell and Yvor Winters. But, even here, a considerable variety of style is possible. Let me put forward three examples. To designate quality, I shall select extracts from critics whom experience has shown me to be particularly useful to students. To maintain focus, I shall choose examples from essays they have written on Shakespeare.

The first is from 'How Many Children Had Lady Macbeth?' (1933) by L. C. Knights. The function of the essay is to show the question – associated with A. C. Bradley's genre of character-analysis – to be meaningless.

Macbeth is a statement of evil. I use the word 'statement' (unsatisfactory as it is) in order to stress those qualities that are 'non-dramatic', if drama is defined according to the canons of William Archer or Dr Bradley. It also happens to be poetry, which means that the apprehension of the whole can only be obtained from a lively attention to the parts, whether they have an immediate bearing on the main action or 'illustrate character', or not. Two main themes, which can only be separated for the purpose of analysis, are blended in the play – the themes of the reversal of values and of unnatural disorder. And closely related to each is a third theme, that of the deceitful appearance, and consequent doubt, uncertainty and confusion. All this is obscured by false assumptions about the category 'drama'; *Macbeth* has greater affinity with *The Waste Land* than with *The Doll's House*...

The second example is from an essay on *As You Like It*, published in 1940 by James Smith. The author is concerned to indicate that many of the same elements occur in comedy as in tragedy; at the same time, he intimates a distinction between the way in which those elements are deployed. This is the (very decisive) start of the essay.

It is a commonplace that Jaques and Hamlet are akin. But it is also a commonplace that Jaques is an intruder into *As You Like It,* so that in spite of the kinship the plays are not usually held to have much connection. I have begun to doubt whether not only *As You Like It* and *Hamlet,* but almost all the comedies and the tragedies as a whole are not closely connected, and in a way which may be quite important.

Recent criticism of Shakespeare has directed itself with profit upon the tragedies, the 'problem plays' and certain of the histories. The early comedies, on the other hand, have either been disparaged or entirely overlooked. Yet the same criticism owes part of its success to a notion of what it calls Shakespeare's 'integrity'; his manifold interests, it has maintained, being co-ordinated so as rarely to thwart, regularly to strengthen, one another. Hence he was alert and active as few have been, while his writing commanded not part but the whole of his resources...

My third example is from *Woe and Wonder* (1951), an essay on the emotional effect of Shakespearean Tragedy, by J. V. Cunningham. At this juncture Cunningham is concerned with the way in which Donatus, a fourth-century follower of Aristotle, redefined the theory of tragedy; especially the belief that tragic characters were essentially figures of high social position.

The first distinction is that the tragic characters must be great, and this means of high rank. It is the modern feeling that this is an artificial stipulation, explicable only in light of the erroneous social ideas of our ancestors. But *The Death of a Salesman* is not a tragedy in the old sense, and so one might conjecture there is something else involved: there is involved a radical difference in the nature of the tragic effect. For the field of tragedy will be the state, since men of high rank are rulers of the state. Tragedy will then involve not private life and private feeling – this is the province of comedy – but public life and public feeling. But public feeling is different in kind from private. A public calamity moves us in a different way than does a private one. The murder of John

Doe is one thing; the assassination of Trotsky or of Admiral Darlan is another. Hence the tragic emotions in the older tradition will be predominantly communal and public, and we will find that a similar qualification is implied in the other principles of order which Donatus distinguishes...

Although these three represent something of a similar order of discourse, there are personal differences. I could not myself mistake the urbane tone of Knights, modestly deprecating his terminology as he goes along, for the more moralistic voice of James Smith. Apart from anything else, the one is, at a great remove, derivative from the late-nineteenth century, the other from the mid-eighteenth. Both of them, further, are quite distinguishable from the tone of J. V. Cunningham. Apart from his greater degree of intensity, he speaks in an American accent. Neither Knights nor Smith would have written: 'A public calamity moves us in a different way than does a private one'. Than does' is an American idiom; though perfectly acceptable, it would not ring true coming from an Englishman. Having said all this, I am also bound to say that there are ideas in common. All three critics are concerned to indicate the way in which a particular kind of poetic tragedy differs from the account of an individual downfall or domestic disaster.

This is a highly acceptable mode of critical discourse. It allows for personal characteristics at the same time as it provides a means of communication between participants in a dialogue. Let me quote two more examples, in a similar vein, from sources not likely to be published.

The 'Problem Plays' are not concerned merely to expose weaknesses of human nature. If that was all they did perhaps only the naive would be disturbed. What is disturbing is their tone, the complexity of the issues they raise and their failure to offer a satisfactory resolution. A play like *Measure for Measure* troubles us because it does not quite 'come off'. Certainly however (without imagining an embittered Jacobean Shakespeare) we must be immediately struck by the disconcertingly bitter tone of these plays. We have black comedy, literally gallows-humour – 'You must rise and be hanged, Master Barnardino' says Pompey in an extraordinary scene in *Measure for Measure* (IV iii 22–23)...

If the reversal of order and the turn of Fortune's wheel was all that lay at the heart of the mature tragedies, they would be much hollower and less agonising than they are. The problem of evil in relation to man, his reactions to it within and without him given a particular set of circumstances and his own changeful nature: the predicament of good in a fallen world – these are also integral parts of Shakespearian tragedy.

In the character of Macbeth for example, these concerns are expressed in the form of paradoxes. Macbeth is a good man: he has real loyalty to Duncan (I iv 22–25), and the milk of human kindness within him, together with his moral scruples outside the banqueting chamber at Inverness and his moral sensitivities before and after the murder reveal his considerable potentialities for good. But always from the same spring comes the other urgency, the divine itch of ambition – I iv 50–53:

> yet let that be
> Which the eye fears, when it is done, to see...

These are taken from two final Honours examination papers written for the university at which I have the privilege of teaching. I am bound to say that not only to myself but to my colleagues these essays seemed worthy of high regard, and both candidates were awarded First Class degrees in English Literature. It is also worth remarking that both these extracts come from the beginning of the essays concerned and so reinforce my contection that one should seek to grip the reader's interest from the outset. While both items are in the same mode, the styles are dissimilar: one would not confuse the formal, epigrammatic manner of the first with the impressionistic and disquisitory manner of the second. They are related, however distantly, the one to Hazlitt, the other to De Quincey.

Yet, when I have said all this, I am conscious of the need to voice a qualification. One recommends these – and Knights, Smith and Cunningham – as examples of critical discourse; but are they great criticism? Isn't there surely, in the end, a lack of zest, audacity, the capacity to disorient and to disturb?

There is; but I cannot suggest that one should inject such qualities into one's prose, even were it possible. Moreover, the audacity whose absence I am implying is more often scorned than applauded. It is the quality that I find in this –

Othello, it will be very generally granted, is of all Shakespeare's great tragedies the simplest: the theme is limited and sharply defined, and the play, everyone agrees, is a brilliantly successful piece of workmanship. The effect is one of a noble 'classical' clarity – of firm, clear outlines, unblurred and undistracted by cloudy recessions, metaphysical aura, or richly symbolical ambiguities. There would, it seems, be something like a consensus in this sense. And yet it is of *Othello* that one can say bluntly, as of no other of the great tragedies, that it suffers in current appreciation an essential and denaturing falsification...

or in this –

Any consideration of the Tragedy of Othello must be primarily occupied, not with its official hero but with its villain. I cannot think of any other play in which only one character performs personal actions— all the *deeds* are Iago's – and all the others without exception only exhibit behaviour. In marrying each other, Othello and Desdemona have performed a deed, but this took place before the play begins. Nor can I think of another play in which the villain is so completely triumphant: everything Iago sets out to do, he accomplishes – (among his goals, I include his self-destruction). Even Cassio, who survives, is maimed for life...

or in this –

I had always felt an aversion from Hamlet: a creeping, unclean thing he seems, on the stage, whether he is Forbes Robertson or anybody else. His nasty poking and sniffing at his mother, his setting traps for the King, his conceited perversion with Ophelia make him always intolerable. The character is repulsive in its conception, based on self-dislike and a spirit of disintegration.

There is, I think, this strain of cold dislike, or self–dislike, through much of the Renaissance art, and through all the later Shakespeare. In Shakespeare it is a kind of corruption in the flesh and a conscious revolt from this. A sense of corruption in the flesh makes Hamlet frenzied, for he will never admit that it is his own flesh. . .

The first two extracts come at the very outset of the essays from which they are quoted, and in many ways I regard all three essays as great criticism. Yet I cannot encourage you to write in this way in the examination room without at the same time warning you of possible calamity. The first extract comes from F. R. Leavis, the same essay as the one in which he attacks Bradley's notion of *Othello* (see Chapter 4); and Leavis had a singularly unfortunate university career, established only in his middle forties. The second extract comes from an essay called 'The Joker in the Pack' (1961) by W. H. Auden; and Auden began *his* career with a Third Class Degree in the Oxford English School, and even now is hardly thought to be the major critic which to my mind he undoubtedly is. The third extract comes from a revision (1915) of an essay on the Theatre in D. H. Lawrence's *Twilight in Italy,* and I cannot find anyone, apart from F. R. Leavis, who considers it to be criticism of any sort, let alone major.

What the extracts from Knights, Smith and Cunningham had in common was the possibility of being accepted; they were discourses, with all their varieties, addressed to the disinterested, reasonable man. By contrast, the essays by Leavis, Auden and Lawrence seem more like shock tactics. We get a sensation of being bombarded by the critic's personality; and, in my view, that is precisely what is happening. More, without the implied presence of a life-long struggle and the availability of the critic's other works, it is unlikely that any of the essays in question would have much credibility. Any one of them would be likely to incur displeasure exposed to the uninstructed eye of the examiner!

Moreover, I am bound to say that, while I personally agree with Leavis on *Othello*, I am aware that many other reasonable people would not. I find Auden on *Othello* entertaining but wrong-headed; and Lawrence on *Hamlet* I believe to be not only a misreading of *Hamlet* in particular but conducive to a misconstruction of Shakespeare at large.

Why, then, do I continue to believe these essays to be important criticism? It is, I suppose, not because they are about Shakespeare but because they are about, respectively, Leavis on Shakespeare, Auden on Shakespeare, Lawrence on Shakespeare. The personality of the critic becomes as central as the integrity of the text. Each critic's reaction to his text is appropriate to him as it would not be to his fellows. Auden's reading of *Othello* is dramatically different from that of Leavis. It is in the wake of A. C. Bradley who believed the play was about the invincible cunning of Iago pitted against the noble Othello. Where Auden's reading differs from that of Bradley is in being much sharper in its response to the text, and that is what it has in common with Leavis, even though it takes Auden in a different direction. This is what we call the first-hand response, and it helps to decide the course of literature.

We read Knights, Smith, Cunningham to some extent to agree with them, and certainly to learn from them about Shakespeare. We read Leavis, Auden, Lawrence to learn about Leavis, Auden, Lawrence. In the process I think we shall learn about Shakespeare, too, but not directly. One's reaction may be negative; we may reply to the onslaught of Lawrence 'no, surely Hamlet was "The glass of fashion and the mould of form"'. However, in formulating our negative we shall, in effect, be frequenting *Hamlet* again. A brilliant tutor might well begin a seminar with some such gesture as that of Lawrence, to get the students to speak, to talk back; essentially, such a seminar would be open-ended. It is what is nowadays called a process of deconstruction: when the critic shows what can be seen in a text rather than what has hitherto been held to be there. For such a critic, the 'hitherto' is less decisive than the 'what can be seen'.

The technique of Knights, Smith and Cunningham, on the other hand, is that of the ordinary decent academic: you will find yourself in his seminars receiving what amounts to a lecture. If Knights voices the fact that *Hamlet* differs from *The Doll's House* or *Death of a Salesman,* no one much is going to disagree with him; there will be singularly little room for comment on the part of the students present. For better or worse, given the formal circumstances of the university, the student writing an essay or sitting an examination is likely to assume that position; to add to the discourse of Knights and Smith, not to astonish the examiner with fireworks displays of wit, with multiple readings of texts, or with analyses based upon irreconcilable paradoxes, as is the way of Leavis, Auden, Lawrence, and, latterly, Barthes and Derrida.

In effect, I have implied that there is no such thing as a model essay. An area of discourse there certainly is, and that discourse is to be initially recommended to the student as that of a teacher expounding a centralized view. At the same time, we must remember that it took some pyromania and bloodshed to get that view across originally, and that is none the less true if the pyres were no more than the rejected drafts of past disquisitions and if the blood shed was that of the pioneering critic. Knights and Smith stand in some degree ancillary to Leavis. A good deal of their best work, creditable as it is, was distilled from hectic discussions when they were graduate students and represents, in all senses, a second phase of activity. I have no doubt that a similar process will take place with regard to the seminar technique of our own day; that the passionate deconstruction by Derrida of the avant-garde story-writer Maurice Blanchot will eventually settle down into discourse of a nature acceptable in tutorial essays. Indeed, there are signs that this is already beginning; in books like *The Critical Difference* by Barbara Johnson and *Structuralism and Since* edited by John Sturrock—useful guides to the frenetic activity among critics of the last twenty years.

The policy of many teachers is essentially that of the contrapuntalist Albrechtsberger, who taught Beethoven. It is necessary to learn to construct fugues before you deconstruct them. An apprenticeship in all forms of traditional metre is perhaps the best foundation for writing free verse. Learning to use the expository mode of conceptual prose will be quite enough to fill your undergraduate years: the fireworks of Leavis, of Auden, of Lawrence, were achieved through a prolonged assemblage of kindling.

Leavis, Auden and Lawrence were sorcerers; the student, while he remains a student, is their apprentice. By the time he has grown up into a mastery of his craft, he will be writing in a manner quite other than theirs. To write like Leavis now would be to wish oneself back in the headily intellectual Cambridge he describes so well in his memoir of Wittgenstein, with its glimpse of W. E. Johnson, the great philosopher's own teacher. We are none of us in a position to speak like 'an established familiar in the little drawing-room, which was a quarter filled with the Broadwood grand on which the old logician used to take his exercise playing Bach'. Not only is the circumstance different from any we are likely to find ourselves in; the style, of necessity, is different, too. A pupil who has learned effectively from his master will be unlikely to copy his externalities: he will not 'cough like Horace'.

It is because of this that we can still read Dryden, Johnson, Coleridge and Arnold, and call them great critics. Nobody is going to imitate their style directly; nobody is going to lose his awareness of the personality and the historical standpoint of the critic he is reading; nobody is going to read such critics simply for guidance on the text. At the same time, the way in which they struggle with their texts in order to formulate their concepts may serve us better than many more straightforward examples of critical discourse; it may, for example, improve our terminology.

So there is no 'ideal essay', no 'working model'; only an area of acceptable discourse through which the student discovers what he responds to and by which he communicates that response. Critical writing leads in many directions. A competent teacher in the field is likely to remember with affection his literary pupils: a scattering of distinguished poets, a leading playwright or two, professors and lecturers in several universities. He may also number among his former pupils a major political figure; an international opera star; senior executives in oil companies; several tax inspectors. Most important of all, his former pupils are bound to include some hundreds of people fulfilling their destinies in unremarkable walks of life. Any competent teacher would like to think that the study of literature – writing about it as well as reading it – in some way had improved their capabilities. After all, we live in a verbal world. As I said at the outset, the training of a critic is also the training of a citizen.

Bibliography

GENERAL

Arnold, Matthew, *Essays in Criticism* (First Series, London, 1865; Second Series, London, 1888)
Coleridge, S. T., *Shakespearean Criticism* (Lectures of 1808, 1811–12, 1812–13, 1818–19, Notes, Marginalia), ed. T. M. Räysor (London, 1960)
– *Biographia Literaria* (1817), ed. G. Watson (London, 1960)
Dryden, John, 'Of Dramatic Poesy: An Essay' (1668), in *Of Dramatic Poesy and Other Critical Essays,* ed. G. Watson (London, 1962)
Eliot, T. S., *The Sacred Wood* (London, 1920)
– *Selected Essays* (London, 1932)
Empson, William, *Seven Types of Ambiguity* (London, 1930, 1949)
Johnson, Samuel, *Lives of the English Poets* (1779–81), rep. Oxford (1905, 1906)
Johnson on Shakespeare (Proposals, 1756; Preface and Notes, 1765; *Rambler* No. 168), ed. W. Raleigh (London, 1908, 1925)
Knight, G. Wilson, *The Wheel of Fire* (London, 1930, 1949)
Leavis, F. R., *Revaluation* (London, 1936)
– *The Great Tradition* (London, 1948)
– *The Common Pursuit* (London, 1952)
Richards, I. A., *Principles of Literary Criticism* (London, 1924)
– *Practical Criticism* (London, 1929)
Winters, Yvor, *In Defense of Reason* (Denver, 1947)
Wordsworth, William, Preface to *Lyrical Ballads* (1800), in *Lyrical Ballads,* ed. R. L. Brett and A. R. Jones (London, 1963)

I THE USE OF CRITICISM

Blackmur, R. P., *Language as Gesture* (London, 1954)
Booth, Wayne C., *The Rhetoric of Fiction* (London, 1961)

Brown, Douglas, *Thomas Hardy* (London, 1954)

Empson, William, *Some Versions of Pastoral* (London, 1935)

Foucault, Michel, *The Order of Things* (1966), tr. anon. (London, 1970) – *The Archaeology of Knowledge* (1962), tr. A. Sheridan (London, 1972)

Freud, Sigmund, 'The Theme of the Three Caskets' (1913), in Works, tr. J. Strachey, XII (London, 1953-66)

Lévi-Strauss, Claude, *The Savage Mind* (1962), tr. anon. (London, 1972)

Marx, Karl, 'Economic and Philosophical Manuscripts' (1844), in *Early Writings,* tr. R. Livingstone and G. Benton (Harmondsworth, Middlesex, 1975)

Mukařovský, Jan, 'Standard Language and Poetic Language' (1932), in *A Prague School Reader,* tr. and ed. P. Garvin (Washington, D. C., 1964)

Russell, Bertrand, *The Problems of Philosophy* (London, 1912)
     The Conquest of Happiness (London, 1930)

Shklovsky, Victor, 'Art as Technique' (1917), in *Russian Formalist Criticism: Four Essays,* tr. L. T. Lemon and M. J. Reis (Lincoln, Nebraska, and London, 1965)

Smith, James, *Shakespearian and other essays* (Cambridge, England, 1974)

Trotsky, Leon, *Literature and Revolution* (1924), tr. R. Strunsky (Ann Arbor, Michigan, 1960)

II WHAT TO SAY ABOUT A POEM

Brown, Douglas, *Thomas Hardy* (London, 1954)

Erlich, Victor, *Russian Formalism: History-Doctrine* (New Haven, Connecticut, and London, 1955, 1965, 1981), especially Chapter XI

Leavis, F. R., *The Living Principle* (London, 1975)

Tynjanov, Juri, 'On Literary Evolution' (1929), in *Readings in Russian Poetics: Formalist and Structural Views,* ed. L. Matejka and K. Pomorska (Massachusetts and London, 1971)

III FOUR MODES OF FICTION

Frye, Northrop, *Anatomy of Criticism: Four Essays* (Princeton, New Jersey, 1957)

Hobsbaum, Philip, *A Theory of Communication* (London, 1970; published as *Theory of Criticism,* Bloomington, Indiana, 1970)

James, Henry, *Critical Prefaces* (1907-09), rep. as *The Art of the Novel,* ed. R. P. Blackmur (New York and London, 1934)

Kinkead-Weekes, Mark, *Samuel Richardson: Dramatic Novelist* (London, 1973)

Leavis, F. R., Klingopulos, G. D., 'The Novel as Dramatic Poem', *Scrutiny* XIV (1946–47), XV (1947–48), etc.
Scholes, Robert and Robert Kellogg, *The Nature of Narrative* (New York and Oxford, 1966)
Woolf, Virginia, *The Common Reader*, First Series (London, 1925)

IV ENGLISH PROSE STYLE

Arnold, Matthew, *Reports on Elementary Schools*, ed. F. Sandford (London, 1889)
Hobsbaum, Philip, *A Theory of Communication* (London, 1970)
James, Henry, 'Honoré de Balzac' (1902), in *Selected Literary Criticism*, ed. M. Shapira (London, 1963)
Lamb, Charles, *Essays of Elia* (1823, 1833), rep. Oxford (1946)
Leavis, F. R., *English Literature in Our Time* (London, 1969)
Ruskin, John, *The Stones of Venice* (1851–52), rep. London (1981)
Russell, Bertrand, 'On Denoting', *Mind* XIV (1905)

V WRITING NOTES

Erskine-Hill, H. H., *The Social Milieu of Alexander Pope* (New Haven, Connecticut, and London, 1975)
Van Ghent, Dorothy, *The English Novel: Form and Function* (New York, 1953)

VI STRUCTURING AN ESSAY

Empson, William, 'Tom Jones', *Kenyon Review* XX (1958), rep. *Henry Fielding*, ed. C. Rawson (Harmondsworth, Middlesex, 1973)
Mukařovský, Jan, 'Standard Language and Poetic Language' (1932), in *A Prague School Reader*, tr. and ed. P. Garvin (Washington, D. C., 1964)
Propp, Vladímir, *Morphology of the Folktale* (1927), tr. L. Scott (Bloomington, Indiana, 1958; Austin, Texas, and London, 1968)
Scholes, Robert, *Structuralism in Literature* (New Haven, Connecticut, and London, 1974)
Van Ghent, Dorothy, *The English Novel: Form and Function* (New York, 1953)

VII BACKGROUND AND BIOGRAPHY

Eliot, T. S., 'Lancelot Andrewes', in *Selected Essays* (London, 1932)

146   BIBLIOGRAPHY

Harding, D. W., 'The Poetry of Wyatt', in *A Guide to English Literature*, ed. B. Ford, I (Harmondsworth, Middlesex, 1954)

Hobsbaum, Philip, *A Reader's Guide to Charles Dickens* (London and New York, 1972)

Nelson, C. E., 'A Note on Wyatt and Ovid', *Modern Language Review* LVIII (1963)

VIII COMPARISON AND ANALYSIS

Cook, Edward, *Florence Nightingale* (London, 1913)

De Quincey, Thomas, *Recollections of the Lake Poets* (1834-40), rep. Harmondsworth, Middlesex (1970)

Hazlitt, William, *The Spirit of the Age* (1825), rep. London (1910)

Hobsbaum, Philip, *Tradition and Experiment in English Poetry* (London and New York, 1979)

Strachey, Lytton, *Eminent Victorians* (1918), rep. Harmondsworth, Middlesex (1971)

IX THE MODEL ESSAY / BREAKING THE MODEL

Auden, W. H., *The Dyer's Hand* (London, 1963)

Barthes, Roland, *Critical Essays* (1964), tr. R. Howard (Evanston, Illinois, 1972)

Bloom, Harold and Paul de Man, Jacques Derrida, et al. *Deconstruction and Criticism* (London, 1979)

Cunningham, J. V., *Tradition and Poetic Structure* (Denver, 1960)

Derrida, Jacques, *Speech and Phenomena* (1976), tr. D. B. Allison (Evanston, Illinois, 1973), esp. translator's introduction

Knights, L. C., *'Hamlet' and other Shakespearean essays* (Cambridge, 1979)

Lawrence, D. H., *Twilight in Italy* (1916), rep. Harmondsworth, Middlesex (1960)

Leavis, F. R., *English Literature in Our Time* (London, 1969)

Norris, Christopher, *Deconstruction: Theory and Practice* (London, 1982)

Smith, James, *Shakespearian and other essays* (Cambridge, England, 1974)

Index

Addison, Joseph 48
'Adventure of the Bruce-Partington Plans,
    The' (Sir Arthur Conan Doyle),
    and influence of Dickens 113
allusion, in poetry 74—8
'ambiguity', in poetry 20
Andrewes, Lancelot, and influence
    on T. S. Eliot 102—4
Antony and Cleopatra
    (William Shakespeare),
    high–mimetic mode in 45
Arnold, Matthew 10, 73, 141
As You Like It
    (William Shakespeare), in an essay
    by James Smith 134
'Atticus' (Alexander Pope) 24—7;
    and see 'The Epistle to Dr Arbuthnot'
Auden, W. H., as critic 137—41
Augustans, Peace of the 24
Austen, Jane 14, 47, 52, 129; and *Pride
    and Prejudice* 36—9; influences
    on 116—23; and *Emma* 120—3

Balzac, Honoré de 62—3
'Belletrist' mode, in non-fiction 53, 54—7
Berkeley, Bishop 49, 50
    Bleak House (Charles Dickens),
    high-mimetic mode in 41—3;
    influences on 104—9; influence
    of 111—2

Bradley, A. C. 60
Brown, Charles Brockden 104
Brown, Douglas 14
Burney, Fanny, and influence of *Evelina*
    on Jane Austen 37—9, 116—23

Carlyle, Thomas 59, 105, 106
Cecil, Lord David 61—2
'centre', of a poem or story 19, 21, 22,
    29, 32, 86; in *Tom Jones* 90—3
Churchill, Sir Winston 59
Clarissa (Samuel Richardson) 39—41
Coleridge, S. T., as critic 10, 141;
    as poet 105
Common Pursuit, The (F. R. Leavis) 60
'concreteness' 13, 83—4
Conrad, Joseph 14
Cook, Sir Edward 125—7
'Copper Beeches, The' (Sir Arthur
    Conan Doyle), and influence
    of Dickens 112
criticism, history of 9—11, 62; nature
    of 11—16; and value judgements 15;
    purpose of 16—17; and different
    modes of fiction 52; and styles
    of critical writing 53—66, 133—42;
    comparison in 111—30; and the
    critic's standpoint 129;
    and the personality
    of the critic 138—9; *and see* poetry,
    criticism of

Cunningham, J. V., and a theory of tragedy 134—5; as an 'acceptable' critic 137, 138, 139, 140

De Quincey, Thomas 123—5
Dickens, Charles 44—5; and *Bleak House* 41—3, 104—9; influence of 111—5
didactic mode 36, 52; in *Pendennis* 46—7
Disraeli, Benjamin 106
Donne, John 49,50
Doyle, Sir Arthur Conan, and Charles Dickens 111, 112—4
Dryden, John, as critic 9—10, 141
'During Wind and Rain' (Thomas Hardy) 28—30, 84

Eliot, George 61
Eliot, T. S., as critic 10, 13; as poet 30—3, 102—4, 113—5
Eminent Victorians (Lytton Strachey) 126—8
Emma (Jane Austen), influences on 120—3
Empson, Sir William 10, 13, 14, 20, 93, 95
English Literature in Our Time (F. R. Leavis) 57—8
'Epistle to Dr Arbuthnot, The' (Alexander Pope) 25, 73—9
essay, structure of an 80—97; techniques in writing an 131—3; styles of 133—42
Evelina (Fanny Burney) 37—9; influence on, and comparison with, *Emma* 116—23
examination questions 81
expository mode, in non-fiction 54, 63—6

fiction, modes of 34—52; key scenes in 69—72
Fielding, Henry 47—8, 85—97

Finnegans Wake (James Joyce) 50
form, analysis of 14
Foucault, Michel 11, 13, 16
Frye, Northrop 35

Golding, William 54
Gordon, George, on T. S. Eliot 115
Grand Style, the 45
Great Tradition, The (F. R. Leavis) 61—2

Hamlet (William Shakespeare), in an essay by D. H. Lawrence 137—8
Hardy, Thomas 28—30, 80—5
Hazlitt, William 123—5
Herbert, George 21—4
high-mimetic mode 35, 47, 84; in *Bleak House* 41—3; in *Macbeth* 42—5; in *Antony and Cleopatra* 45
Historical Intentionalism 10
history, and literature 125—9

impressionist mode 36, 48; in *Jacob's Room* 49; in *Ulysses* 49—50; in *Tristram Shandy* 50—2; attack on 63—4
influences, on writers 98—110; study of, for comparison 111—30
ironic mode, in non-fiction 54, 60—3

Jacob Faithful (Captain Marryat) 105
Jacob's Room (Virginia Woolf), impressionist mode in 49
James, Henry 14, 62—3, 66
Johnson, Samuel, as critic 141
'Journey of the Magi, The' (T. S. Eliot) 30—3; provenance of 102—4
Joyce, James 36, 49—50

'key scenes' 69—72
Knight, G. Wilson 14

Knights, L. C., and *Macbeth* 133; as an 'acceptable' critic 135, 137, 138, 139, 140

Lamb, Charles 56, 66
language, analysis of 13—14; in poetry 23—4, 29; in key scenes 72
Lawrence, D. H., as critic 137—41
Leavis, F. R. 10, 11, 13, 14, 35, 63, 66; as 'Prophet' 57—8; as 'Ironist' 59—61; and *Othello* 60—1, 137—8; and George Eliot 61—2; and *Tom Jones* 86; and T. S. Eliot 115; and the personality of the critic 138—41
Lévi-Strauss, Claude 10—11, 13, 16
Lillo, George 40—1
literacy, importance of 59
'Logs on the Hearth' (Thomas Hardy) 84—5
London Merchant, The (George Lillo) 40—1
Lord of the Flies (William Golding) 54, 55
'Love-Song of J. Alfred Prufrock, The' (T. S. Eliot) 113—5
low-mimetic mode 35, 47; in *Pride and Prejudice* 36—8, 116

Macbeth (William Shakespeare), high-mimetic mode in 43—5; in an essay by L. C. Knights 133
Marlowe, Christopher, and translation of Ovid 100—2
Marryat, Captain 105
Melville, Herman 105
metrical structure, in Thomas Hardy's poems 81
moral considerations, in criticism 95—6
Morris, William 59
Mukařovský, Jan 13

non-fiction, modes of 53—66
notes, in literary criticism 68, 74, 75, 76, 77, 79

Odyssey (Homer) 45—6
Othello (William Shakespeare) 60—1; in essays by Leavis and Auden 137—8
Ovid, and influence on Sir Thomas Wyatt 99—102; Marlowe translation 100—2

Pendennis (W. M. Thackeray) 46—7
plot, in *Pride and Prejudice* 68—72; in *Tom Jones* 88
poetry, criticism of 18—34, 72—9, 80—5; memorizing of 73
Pope, Alexander 24—7, 74—9
Pound, Ezra 115
Pride and Prejudice (Jane Austen), low-mimetic mode in 36—8; and *Evelina* 39; plot in 68—72
Primitivism and Decadence (Yvor Winters) 63—5
'prophetic' mode, in non-fiction 53, 57—9
Propp, Vladimir, and an approach to *Tom Jones* 86—90
prose *see* fiction; non-fiction
'Pulley, The' (George Herbert) 21—4
Pyramid, The (William Golding) 54, 55

reading, as a technique 67; and re-reading 95
'Recollections of the Lake Poets' (Thomas De Quincey) 123—5
Redburn (Herman Melville) 105
rhythm, in poetry 27, 29, 82
Richards, I. A. 10, 13; and T. S. Eliot 115
Richardson, Samuel 39—41, 116
Ruskin, John 58—9
Russell, Bertrand 11, 65—6

'Self-Unseeing, The' (Thomas Hardy)
83—4

Shakespeare, William 14, 41;
and *Macbeth* 43—5; and styles
of criticism of 133—9

Shklovsky, Victor 13

Sidney, Sir Philip 9

Sign of Four, The (Sir Arthur Conan
Doyle), and influence of Dickens 112

Sir Charles Grandison (Samuel
Richardson) influence on, and
comparison with, *Emma* 116—8

Smith, James 14; and *As You Like It*
133—4; as an 'acceptable' critic 135,
137, 138, 139, 140

Spirit of the Age, The
(William Hazlitt) 123—5

Squire, Sir John, and 'The Waste Land'
(T. S. Eliot) 115—6

Steele, Richard 48

Sterne, Laurence 36, 50—2

Stevens, Wallace 81

Stones of Venice, The
(John Ruskin) 58—9

Strachey, Lytton 126—8

'stream of consciousness' 50, 51, 63—4

Structuralism 10—11

structure, analysis of 14, 28—30, 67—8;
in *Tom Jones* 86—90

summary, making a 68—78, 85—6

Sybil (Benjamin Disraeli) 106

symbolism, in 'The Journey of the Magi'
31—2; in *Bleak House* 105—8

Thackeray, W. M. 46—7

'They flee from me' (Sir Thomas Wyatt)
18—21; provenance of 98—102

Tom Jones (Henry Fielding), and the
didactic mode 47—8; approaches to
86—97; a classic 94—5

tone, analysis of 25

tradition, in literature 116

tragedy, in *Othello* 60—1; in an essay
by J. V. Cunningham 134—5; in
essays by Leavis and Auden 137

Tristram Shandy (Laurence Sterne) 36;
impressionist mode in 50—2

Ulysses (James Joyce), impressionist
mode in 49—50

value judgements, in criticism *see*
criticism, and value judgements

Van Ghent, Dorothy 90

Vanity Fair (W. M. Thackeray) 47

verbal analysis *see* language, analysis of

'Voices from Things Growing in
a Churchyard' (Thomas Hardy) 82

Wilson Knight, G. 14

Winters, Yvor 13, 14, 66; and the
expository mode 63—5

Woolf, Virginia 34, 49

Wordsworth, William, as critic 10;
descriptions of, by De Quincey
and Hazlitt 123—5

Wyatt, Sir Thomas 18—21, 98—102